The Spice Kitchen

This book is dedicated to my husband Chris, who teaches me something new each day.
Without him, nothing would be possible.
Thank you, Chris, for your long-suffering love and patience. MH

To my parents Judy and Peter Blanchard,
thank you for your love, support and encouragement –
you are my "rock solids" JB

The Spice Kitchen

Flavorful Recipes From Around the World

michal haines

photography by jacqui blanchard

Interlink Books

An imprint of Interlink Publishing Group, Inc.
Northampton, Massachusetts
www.interlinkbooks.com

Contents

Welcome to My Kitchen

For me, the words "Silk Road" and "Spice Trail" conjure up evocative images of another time when men risked their lives journeying across oceans and unknown lands to satisfy the palates of their kings and queens. The romantic notions that spices evoke in me are bound intrinsically with discovery. I imagine the first adventurer to reach the Amazon and taste cinnamon and cocoa; the first man to sit at the king's table and sample a whole new realm of heavenly delights rich with cumin, coriander, and cardamom.

For us in our kitchens, centuries later, spices make it possible to travel far and wide on a culinary plane, gaining fascinating insights into other cultures along the way. Spices also open up an extra dimension in cooking that can transform dishes from ordinary to sublime.

This book came about because spices – their intense flavors and the way they have influenced and subsequently been absorbed into the cuisines of the world – have long fascinated me. In my own kitchen, experimentation reigns supreme. My own culinary background is as much about the discovery of flavors as it is about the knowledge I have acquired.

My culinary investigations and fascination with flavor began as a small child. My Chinese grandfather Stan, or Aghung as we called him, was a consummate chef and watching him cook counts among my fondest childhood memories. Dressed for a Siberian winter, no matter what time of year it was, his preparation would begin with the ritual rolling up of his plaid shirt sleeves and long johns. He was a master of the cleaver, using two cleavers to mince meat in the most rhythmical manner. I remember sitting on the back steps of our house, listening to the thump of his cleavers, anticipating the treats in store. I have one of his cleavers in my kitchen today and while I am not nearly skilled enough to work his kind of magic with it, it is a reminder of where it all began for me.

My grandfather's early influence had a number of positive outcomes, not least of which was the fact that unusual ingredients and cooking methods have never daunted me.

Spices provide a wealth of opportunities for the cook who loves to experiment. Over the years my kitchen has played the role of home base while I traveled the world of different cuisines via spices, learning about their unique roles in different culinary traditions. This book is the next stage of that journey for me – the opportunity to share my knowledge of spices with you. I hope that as well as cooking the recipes within these pages, you will also be inspired to invent your own flavorsome dishes. Then you too will navigate a journey of discovery through the world of spices.

❈ Cooking With Spices

Learning how to identify, blend, and cook with spices can truly blow your pantry doors wide open. To make things as easy and practical as possible, any one of the following tools will help you get started:

MORTAR AND PESTLE
A mortar and pestle is useful for grinding and pulping spices as well as making spice pastes. It consists of a heavy bowl made of marble, stone or earthenware (mortar) and a solid blunt-ended stick (pestle) usually made of a similar material. It is also ideal for making pesto, aïoli, and other sauces so choose a good-sized one.

HAND GRATER / MICROPLANE
A hand grater is a small, one-sided, rectangular grater with a handle that – as the name suggests – is able to be held while grating (rather than sitting upright on the bench like the traditional three-sided grater). A hand grater is much less cumbersome than the three-sided version, not least because you can grate directly into your pan. A microplane, on the other hand, is even better than a hand grater because, if treated well, it will stay sharp forever. The microplane resembles a long carpentry file. Its razor-sharp blade is ideal for grating spices as well as zesting citrus fruit and grating hard cheeses.

ELECTRICAL SPICE GRINDER
Spice grinders are fast and efficient, but the key is to make sure they are wiped out well after use to avoid flavor contaminations. Often marketed as "coffee and spice grinders," I would recommend buying one exclusively for grinding spices rather than coffee also.

>‒+◆+‒०‒+◆+‒<

Spices fall into five distinct categories. It is important to bear these categories in mind when you're experimenting:

SWEET
These are the spices often included in cakes, puddings, milk desserts, and pastries. The taste of vanilla, king of spices, is easily recognizable and sits with cinnamon on its right hand and cassia on the left. Other commonly used sweet spices are nutmeg and allspice.

PUNGENT
Astringent, with bold character, pungent spices can provide that x-factor. Fenugreek seed and liquorice, mace, cardamom, clove, cumin, juniper, ginger, and star anise fall into this category. But they are like the naughty children at a birthday party in that if allowed to dominate, they will. Use sparingly.

TANGY
Tangy spices lift and freshen the flavor of a dish in the same way that a squeeze of lemon can provide the perfect finishing touch. Sumac and tamarind are two good examples of this.

HOT
Hot spices don't have to result in a teary-eyed reaction. Used sparingly, a spice such as chili, which stimulates the taste buds to release endorphins, can add a whole new dimension to many dishes. Hot spices can be addictive, however, so try not to fuel the addiction as too much hot spice can "burn out" your taste buds, affecting your ability to taste other ingredients.

AMALGAMATING
The following wonderfully versatile spices can almost be used in any amount without being overpowering: coriander seed, fennel seed, sesame seed, poppy seed, and turmeric. They are very good staples to start with when establishing a "spice chest."

Use the following tips as a guide for making your own spice blends. If you think about the flavor combinations and how they might work with the other ingredients you have in mind, you are halfway towards creating new dishes of your own. Remember to keep a record of your blends and quantities so you can successfully recreate them next time.

INDIAN CUISINE

Most people tend to associate Indian food with hot spices when in fact some of the more mellow spices are also often found in Indian food. Examples of spices common to Indian cuisine are coriander seed, turmeric, cinnamon, cumin, fenugreek, ginger, pepper, chili, cloves, tamarind, cardamom, and saffron.

NORTH AFRICAN CUISINE

Moroccan dishes often incorporate combinations of the following spices: coriander, turmeric, paprika, cumin, cinnamon, ginger, cloves, pepper, and chili. Neighboring countries such as Egypt and Algeria also incorporate allspice, ginger, and fenugreek into their particular cuisines.

MIDDLE EASTERN CUISINE

In the Middle East, the hot weather is counter-balanced on the tongue through the tangy flavors of sumac, oily thyme, cassia, cloves, and cinnamon as well as pepper and chili.

ASIAN CUISINE

Indonesian cuisine features lemongrass alongside galangal and ginger, turmeric, and cumin. In Thailand, kaffir lime leaves, cilantro, and green chili are prominent. Chinese dishes often include cinnamon, star anise, Szechuan peppercorns, fennel, and ginger. Japanese food, by contrast, is notably lacking in spices although black sesame seeds do feature and the condiment wasabi is served alongside sweet pickles and seafood.

MEXICAN CUISINE

Mexican dishes are a wonderful mixture of styles and flavors, many of which have been "borrowed" from other cultures. Cilantro, chili, paprika, and musky oregano are the most common herbs and spices to be found in this cuisine.

>⊹⧫⊹O⊹⧫⊹<

If you are serious about building a spice chest that will enable you to tackle any of the cuisines of the world, the following are essential. For more comprehensive information about spices, please see the Spice Glossary (page 183).

- Allspice berries
- Amchur
- Aniseed (ground)
- Bay leaves
- Caraway
- Cardamom (green and brown)
- Cassia bark
- Chilies (dried)
- Cinnamon (sticks and ground)
- Cloves (whole)
- Coriander seeds
- Cumin seeds
- Fennel seeds
- Fenugreek seeds
- Juniper berries
- Kokum
- Mace blades
- Mustard seeds (black and yellow)
- Nutmeg
- Paprika (Spanish smoked sweet, bitter-sweet, Hungarian, and hot)
- Peppercorns (pink, black, white, and Szechuan)
- Saffron
- Sesame seeds
- Star anise
- Sumac
- Vanilla pods

Mezze

A taste, a nibble, a shared plate – mezze has become so popular that terms such as "tapas" and "antipasto" are regularly seen on café and restaurant menus everywhere.

Mezze is a wonderful way of introducing friends to new spice combinations. A successful mezze contains a variety of little taste explosions so that people can sample several flavors in one sitting. Enjoy great mezze with well-matched drinks and friends.

✲ Spiced Spanish Squid

Serves 6–10 as part of a tapas feast

This is a very simple recipe and the spice base can be used for anything that you think may suit the deep-fried treatment.

    1 lb squid, cleaned and cut into pieces
    grapeseed oil for frying
    2⅓ cups ground almonds
    2 teaspoons Spanish smoked sweet paprika
    2 teaspoons salt
    2 tablespoons whole coriander seeds, toasted and finely ground
    2 teaspoons freshly ground black pepper
    2 teaspoons whole allspice berries, finely ground
    zest of 2 limes
    2 eggs, beaten

1. Pat dry the squid.

2. Heat a deep fryer to 350°F/190°C. Alternatively, heat enough grapeseed oil in a frying pan for shallow frying.

3. Combine the dry ingredients and lime zest in a bowl or plastic bag. Place the beaten egg in a separate bowl. Dip the squid into the beaten egg, a few pieces at a time, then into the dry mix. If you are using a plastic bag, add all the squid then shake the bag about to evenly coat the squid.

4. Fry the squid in small batches for about 2 minutes, taking care not to overcrowd the pan, until brown and crisp.

5. Drain on paper towels and serve with an aïoli as part of a finger-food experience.

NOTE: See page 75 for instructions about preparing fresh squid.

✲ Heavenly Haloumi

Serves 2–3 (or 1 very hungry person)

Traditionally made with a mix of goat's, cow's, and sheep's milk, haloumi should always be cooked. A good haloumi should grill or fry without becoming gooey. The mouth feel should be springy and it might even make a slight squeak in your mouth when you bite into it.

    1 tablespoon grapeseed oil
    7 oz haloumi, drained, and cut into ½-inch cubes
    1 teaspoon sea salt
    2 teaspoons ground sumac
    1 tablespoon toasted cumin seeds
    ⅓ cup chopped fresh mint
    juice of 1 lemon
    3 tablespoons extra virgin olive oil

1. Heat the grapeseed oil in a frying pan. When hot, add enough cubes of haloumi to make a single layer in the pan and fry until golden brown. Flip over the haloumi and repeat the process. Drain on paper towels, but if it looks too gooey simply place straight onto a serving platter. Sprinkle with the sea salt, sumac, cumin seeds, and mint and drizzle with lemon juice and olive oil.

2. Serve immediately as part of a mezze.

🦁 Catalan Black Pudding

Serves 4 as part of a tapas spread or 2 as a main meal

The flavors of cinnamon, cloves, and nutmeg feature in the Catalan version of black pudding, known as *morcilla*. Buy a black pudding with a grainy texture to complement the other ingredients. Serve as part of a tapas spread, with extra salad vegetables, or for brunch.

    1 x 14 oz can chickpeas
    1 tablespoon grapeseed oil
    2 cloves garlic, peeled and finely chopped
    ½ red onion, peeled and finely sliced
    5 oz black pudding, coarsely chopped
    2 teaspoons Spanish bitter-sweet smoked paprika
    2 tablespoons finely chopped Italian (flat-leaf) parsley
    2 tablespoons toasted pine nuts
    1 oz sultanas or golden raisins, soaked in hot water for 20 minutes then drained well
    sea salt and freshly ground black pepper
    1 lemon, cut into wedges

1. Drain and rinse the chickpeas, then set aside in a colander to drain completely.

2. Heat the oil in a large frying pan and fry the garlic and onion until they start to brown. Add the black pudding to the pan and cook for a few minutes until it turns crisp. Stir in the paprika and parsley and mix well. Finally, add the chickpeas, pine nuts, and sultanas or golden raisins. Serve on a platter sprinkled with the salt and pepper and lemon wedges.

🦁 Summer Barbecued Duck

Serves 4

Summer is the time to break out the barbecue and produce those all-too-familiar aromas of charred meat. An interesting variation on the standard gas barbecue is the spit roast – all you need is an open fire with some hot embers. Consider enjoying this dish at the beach after a long day in the sun. Ask your local butcher to remove the bones from the meat so it skewers a little more easily.

    2 whole mace blades, toasted very lightly for 10 seconds and then crushed
    4 star anise
    6 juniper berries, crushed but still whole
    3 tablespoons honey
    3 sprigs fresh thyme
    3 tablespoons grapeseed oil
    salt and freshly ground black pepper
    4 duck legs, washed and patted dry
    8 large shallots, peeled

1. Mix together the first seven ingredients. Add the duck to the bowl and massage the marinade into the skin. Allow to marinate overnight, if possible, or for at least 3 hours.

2. Thread each duck leg onto a long metal skewer with a shallot at each end and roast over hot embers, turning regularly and basting with the marinade as you go, for about 20 minutes. Allow to cool slightly before removing the cooked meat from the skewers and eating.

🦁 Spiced Asparagus Dip

This dip is wonderful served with fresh ciabatta, flat bread, or lavash-style crispbread.

6 cloves garlic, roasted in their skins
½ cup frozen peas, defrosted
½ cup frozen fava beans, defrosted and skins removed
2 bunches fresh young asparagus, blanched and refreshed in cold water, then finely chopped
2 spring onions, finely chopped
1 small baby fennel, finely chopped
2 anchovies (optional)
10 green olives, pitted
2 sprigs fresh mint
handful of fresh Italian (flat-leaf) parsley
1 teaspoon fennel seeds, toasted and finely ground
1 teaspoon cumin seeds, toasted and finely ground
juice of ½ lemon
olive oil

1. Remove the skins from the roasted garlic cloves. Place in a food processor along with all the other ingredients except the olive oil and process until a lovely green coarsely textured paste is formed. Slowly add the olive oil through the feed tube so the paste remains nice and thick and still has some texture.

2. Serve in a bowl with the bread of your choice and perhaps some other delicious mezze treats.

🦁 Spice-crusted Peanut Nibbles

Serves 4

Delightful to enjoy alongside a cold beer. Look for chickpea flour (also called besan flour or just pea flour) at Indian specialty stores and health food shops.

3 teaspoons toasted cumin seeds
3 tablespoons chickpea flour
3 Kashmiri chilies, seeded and finely chopped
1 teaspoon ground turmeric
2 teaspoons coriander seeds, toasted and lightly ground
3 teaspoons black mustard seeds
3 teaspoons fennel seeds, toasted
2 teaspoons salt
5 tablespoons water
3 cups raw peanuts with skins on
grapeseed oil for frying

1. Finely grind half the cumin seeds. Set aside with the unground cumin seeds.

2. Mix together the chickpea flour with the next seven ingredients to form a thin paste. It may take up to about a cup of water to make the mixture thin enough so that it coats the peanuts but doesn't clump them together too much. Add the peanuts to the mixture and stir to coat.

3. Heat a wok or deep frying pan with enough grapeseed oil to deep-fry the peanuts. Fry the peanuts, in batches, for 2 minutes at a time. As they cook, they will form little fritters which can be broken up once cooked or served as is.

4. Sprinkle over the cumin. Drain on paper towels and eat right away, taking care not to burn your fingers or tongue.

🦁 Chicken Livers with Szechuan Peppercorns and Pears

Serves 2 for a fast meal

Unusually, the seeds in Szechuan pepper are discarded rather than the husk or pod. Preparing them yourself can be a little time consuming so watch out for Szechuan pepper packaged without seeds at Asian supermarkets or specialty stores.

3 tablespoons whole Szechuan peppercorns, ground
2 tablespoons finely ground polenta
1 tablespoon all-purpose flour
2 fresh pears of your choice, peeled, cored, and cut into segments
3 tablespoons Spanish sherry vinegar
1 tablespoon superfine sugar
juice of ½ lemon
2 tablespoons grapeseed oil
5 oz chicken livers, well washed, drained, and membranes removed
1 teaspoon sea salt
½ teaspoon freshly ground black pepper
arugula leaves to serve

1. Preheat the oven to 350°F/180°C.

2. Combine the Szechuan pepper with the polenta and flour in a shallow bowl. Set aside.

3. Place the pears in a baking dish. Pour over the sherry vinegar, then sprinkle the pears with the sugar and finally the lemon juice.

4. Bake for 10–15 minutes or until soft. Remove the dish from the oven and set aside to cool.

5. Heat the oil in a large frying pan. Coat each liver in the flour mix, then fry until golden brown and cooked to your liking. Season, then toss the cooked pears, arugula leaves, and livers in the remaining juice from the pears and arrange on a serving platter.

6. Serve with thick slices of toasted bread.

🐾 Living Dead Stuffed Chilies

Serves 6 as part of a feasting extravaganza

In Mexico, the Day of the Dead is a special occasion for family and friends. Food is symbolically laid out for the dead to feast upon. The food is said to give the spirits positive energy, which is shared by the living when they eat the same food.

STUFFING
12 medium-sized mild chilies, preferably poblano
2 tablespoons grapeseed oil
1 red onion, peeled and finely chopped
3 cloves garlic, peeled and finely chopped
1 teaspoon ground allspice
1 teaspoon ground cinnamon
1 lb ground free-range pork
1 tablespoon raisins
grated zest of 1 lemon
3 tablespoons chopped almonds
6 tablespoons chopped fresh mint
3 teaspoons chopped fresh cilantro
¼ nutmeg, freshly grated
4 tomatoes, chopped
1 teaspoon salt
¼ teaspoon freshly ground black pepper

BATTER
4 large eggs, separated
1 teaspoon salt
all-purpose flour

grapeseed oil for frying
5 oz crème fraîche
seeds from 2 ripe pomegranates

1. Preheat the oven to 400°F/200°C.

2. Place the chilies in a roasting dish and rub each with a little of the oil. Roast for 10 minutes or until softened. Remove from the oven and allow to cool.

3. Make a small incision in the side of each chili and remove the seeds and "rib" (wear gloves to do this).

4. Heat the remaining oil in a large frying pan and cook the onion and garlic for 2–3 minutes until softened. Stir in the allspice and cinnamon, then add the ground pork and cook until brown, breaking up the meat with a fork if necessary. Add the remaining ingredients and cook for 10 minutes. Add 1 tablespoon of water if the mixture gets too dry and starts to stick. Remove from the heat and set aside to cool.

5. Stuff the mixture into the chilies, handling them with great care to avoid ripping the skins.

6. Make the batter. Beat the egg whites with the salt until soft peaks have formed.

7. Beat the yolks in a separate bowl. Gently fold in the whites.

8. Roll the stuffed chilies in a little flour, then dip each one into the egg mixture.

9. Heat the grapeseed oil. Fry the battered chilies in batches until golden and slightly puffed up. Drain on paper towels.

10. Serve with crème fraîche on the side and scattered with the pomegranate seeds.

🪺 Istanbul Street Mussels

Serves 4 as a meal or 6 as part of a mezze

Served hot or cold as part of a mezze, this mussel dish is an adaptation of what you might find on a street corner in Istanbul. Leftovers can be eaten the next day cold with flatbread and relish.

3 tablespoons grapeseed oil
2 red onions, peeled and finely chopped
5 cloves garlic, peeled and finely chopped
2 teaspoons tomato paste
2 tablespoons fresh pomegranate seeds or currants soaked in water for 15 minutes
2 teaspoons ground allspice
1 teaspoon ground cinnamon
1 teaspoon whole fennel seeds, toasted and finely ground
4 whole cloves
2 bay leaves
⅘ cup white short-grain rice, rinsed well
1 teaspoon salt
½ teaspoon freshly ground black pepper
⅓ cup well washed, roughly chopped fresh cilantro
3 tablespoons well washed, roughly chopped fresh dill
2 tablespoons pine nuts, toasted
40 large fresh mussels
lemon wedges and freshly chopped dill to garnish

1. Heat the oil in a heavy-based frying pan with a lid. Cook the onion and garlic for 2 minutes or until softened. Add the tomato paste, pomegranate seeds (or currants), spices, and bay leaves, stirring well. Add the rice, stirring to coat. Add enough water to cover the rice by ¾ inch, then cover, reduce heat to a simmer and cook for 15 minutes.

2. Remove the pan from the heat. Cool, then fluff up the rice, removing and discarding the cloves and bay leaves. Season to taste, then stir through the chopped herbs and pine nuts, mixing well.

3. Place the mussels in a large saucepan or stockpot with plenty of water. Bring to a boil and transfer the mussels as they start to open into a sinkful of cold water. Discard any that do not open. (If you have any doubts about a half-opened mussel, just throw it away. You will have enough to spare.)

4. Force open each mussel and spoon in enough of the rice mix to fill, then squeeze them shut. Pack the stuffed mussels into a colander or steamer and position over a saucepan half-filled with water. Weight the mussels with a large stone or heavy lid, then cover. Bring the water to a boil, then simmer for 15 minutes before removing and arranging into either one large bowl or several smaller bowls. Serve with lemon wedges and sprinkle with freshly chopped dill.

✣ Old-fashioned Spanish Chicken

Serves 2-3

A Spanish dish that harks from the 17th century and which features lemon and ginger.
A winning concoction that can be enjoyed at any time of year.

  4 tablespoons toasted pine nuts plus 2 tablespoons extra to garnish
  sea salt and pepper to taste
  1 teaspoon saffron threads
  3 tablespoons freshly chopped Italian (flat-leaf) parsley
  2 teaspoons toasted cumin seeds
  2 chicken thighs
  3 tablespoons grapeseed oil
  1 medium red onion, peeled and finely chopped
  3 cloves garlic, peeled and finely chopped
  1 cup chicken stock
  2 bay leaves
  grated zest and juice of 2 lemons
  1½-inch piece ginger root, peeled and finely grated

1. Grind together the pine nuts and 1 teaspoon of sea salt, the pepper, saffron, parsley, and cumin seeds to a paste consistency in a mortar and pestle.

2. Cut the chicken thighs into pieces. Heat a little of the oil in a frying pan and brown the chicken. Remove from the pan and set aside.

3. Using the same pan, brown the onion and garlic. Add the spice paste to the pan, followed by the cooked chicken and stir together well. Pour in the chicken stock, add the bay leaves, lemon, and ginger and reduce the heat. Simmer for 15–20 minutes or until the chicken is cooked.

4. Lift out the chicken and set aside to cool. Reduce the liquid if desired. Taste and adjust seasoning if necessary.

5. Remove the chicken meat from the bones and return it to the sauce to heat through.

6. Serve on rice with a side of salad greens or steamed green beans garnished with the extra toasted pine nuts.

Mid-week Speed

When time constraints and fatigue get the best of you, the quick and easy recipes in this chapter will help keep stress at bay. Spices are easy to work with in the kitchen and they so easily transform the everyday to the truly delicious. Interesting flavors shouldn't just be reserved for weekends and special occasions.

🦁 Watermelon, Cumin Seed, and Feta Salad

Serves 3–4

Serve this salad alongside grilled fish or poultry for a healthy meal. Look for good-quality feta that is quite textured and dry rather than soft and creamy.

½ large watermelon, rind cut off, seeded, and cut into thin slices
1 red onion, peeled and finely sliced
2 teaspoons toasted cumin seeds
7 oz dry sheep's milk feta, finely sliced
1 bunch pea sprouts or arugula leaves
4 tablespoons toasted pistachio kernels
3 tablespoons extra virgin olive oil
freshly ground black pepper

1. Mix together in a large bowl all the ingredients except the oil and pepper, reserving some cumin seeds and pistachio kernels to sprinkle on top. Drizzle the oil over, then scatter over the remaining seeds and kernels along with some black pepper.

🦁 Cornmeal-jacketed Fish with Saffron and Grape Salsa

Serves 4

The wonderful texture and nutty flavor of cornmeal makes a great coating for fish. Kids will eat it and it is also ideal for anyone who is gluten-intolerant. Adding ground nuts gives the coating even more flavor. Experiment with different nuts and fish.

SALSA
1 mild red onion, peeled and finely chopped
2 cloves garlic, peeled and finely chopped
1 mild red chili, seeded and finely chopped
handful of Italian (flat-leaf) parsley, finely chopped
12 grapes, green or black, halved with seeds removed
1 teaspoon saffron threads, lightly toasted then crushed
3 tablespoons Spanish sherry vinegar
4 tablespoons Spanish extra virgin olive oil

FISH
4 white fish filets
⅓ cup cornmeal
⅛ cup macadamia nuts, ground in a food processor or mortar and pestle
1 teaspoon salt
1 teaspoon freshly ground black pepper
2 eggs, beaten
grapeseed oil for frying

1 romaine lettuce, well washed

1. Make the salsa first. Combine all the ingredients in a bowl and allow to sit for 10–20 minutes to infuse.
2. Wash and pat dry the fish. Mix together the cornmeal, nuts, salt, and pepper.
3. Heat the oil in a frying pan. Dip each filet first in the beaten egg, then in the cornmeal and fry each side over medium heat for 3–4 minutes until golden brown.
4. Serve immediately with some salsa spooned over each filet on lettuce leaves.

🦁 *Mid-week Falafel*

Serves 4

These tasty little balls are fast to make and can be eaten as finger food or stuffed into pita bread with feta and greens for lunch or dinner. Baking rather than frying makes them that much healthier and you can relax with a book or magazine while they cook.

1½ cups frozen fava beans, defrosted in a little cold water and skins removed
2 x 14 oz cans chickpeas, rinsed well and drained
6 tablespoons fresh mint leaves, washed and finely chopped
2 tablespoons cilantro leaves, washed and finely chopped
4 cloves garlic, peeled
2 teaspoons toasted cumin seeds
2 teaspoons whole coriander seeds, toasted and ground
finely grated zest and juice of 1 lemon
2 teaspoons baking powder
¼ cup chickpea flour
1 teaspoon salt
½ teaspoon freshly ground black pepper
½ cup sesame seeds

1. Preheat the oven to 350°F/180°C.
2. Combine all the ingredients except the sesame seeds in a food processor or blender. Blend until smooth.
3. Using wet hands, form tablespoon-sized balls of the falafel mix.
4. Pour out the sesame seeds onto a plate. Roll the balls in the sesame seeds to coat.
5. Place in a greased oven dish and bake for 15 minutes, occasionally shaking the dish so the balls brown evenly.
6. Serve with plain or marinated feta slices, baby spinach or other salad greens, and a spoonful of Patient Date and Lemon Chutney (see page 178).

Andalusian Fish with Eggplant Cake

Serves 4

Polenta is a useful grain to have in the cupboard, not least because it adds texture and taste to dishes like this. If you can prepare the eggplant cake the day before, you'll be able to put this dish together in no time.

EGGPLANT CAKE

2 large eggplants, thinly sliced
2 large potatoes, peeled and thinly sliced
6 tablespoons grapeseed oil
2 tablespoons butter
1 leek, well washed and finely sliced
4 cloves garlic, peeled and finely chopped
1⅛ cups half & half
2 eggs
1 teaspoon salt
½ teaspoon freshly ground black pepper
½ nutmeg, freshly grated
4 tablespoons coarsely ground polenta

FISH

1 teaspoon whole cloves
1 tablespoon fennel seeds
2 tablespoons finely chopped oregano leaves
1 teaspoon salt
1 tablespoon Spanish smoked sweet paprika
1 tablespoon Spanish sherry vinegar
1 cup all-purpose flour
½ teaspoon freshly ground black pepper
8 trevally filets (or any other firm, white-fleshed fish), skin on
3 tablespoons grapeseed oil
fresh oregano leaves to garnish, roughly chopped

1. Preheat the oven to 350°F/180°C.

2. Toss the eggplant and potato slices in the oil (best done in a plastic bag), then place the coated slices in a large baking dish. Bake for 20 minutes or until the eggplant has started to brown and the potatoes have softened.

3. Meanwhile, heat the butter in a frying pan and cook the leek and garlic for 4–5 minutes until they are well softened.

4. Once the potato and eggplant are cooked and softened, grease a shallow baking dish or tart pan and arrange the eggplant, potato, leek, and garlic in layers. Whisk together the half & half, eggs, salt, pepper, and nutmeg. Pour the mixture over the layered vegetables, lifting slices here and there to allow it to seep through. Sprinkle the polenta over the top and bake for 20 minutes or until browned on top. The eggplant cake can be made a day ahead if you like. To reheat, simply place in an oven preheated to 350°F/180°C for 35 minutes.

5. To prepare the fish, grind together the cloves, fennel seeds, oregano, and salt in a mortar and pestle. Transfer the mixture to a bowl and add the paprika, sherry vinegar, flour, and pepper, mixing well.

6. Make 3–4 slits on each filet so that they cook through evenly. Coat the filets in the spice and flour mixture.

7. Heat the oil in a frying pan and fry the filets, in batches, for about 3 minutes on each side.

8. Serve with a hot slice of eggplant cake sprinkled with fresh oregano.

Buffalo Mozzarella Fritters with Red Salad

Serves 1 (because it is just too good to share)

The delicate taste of buffalo mozzarella is hard to beat. In fact, it is almost criminal to do anything to it other than slice it and scoff it, but this is a nice simple compromise. For a vegetarian option, simply omit the anchovies.

FRITTERS
9 oz buffalo mozzarella, drained and torn into small pieces
finely grated zest of ½ lemon
2 tablespoons freshly chopped Italian (flat-leaf) parsley, plus 2 tablespoons extra whole leaves to garnish
2 teaspoons whole fennel seeds, toasted and coarsely ground
1 cup freshly made sourdough breadcrumbs
6 tablespoons all-purpose flour
2 teaspoons baking powder
6 tablespoons milk
1 egg, lightly beaten
½ teaspoon salt
¼ teaspoon freshly ground black pepper
grapeseed oil for frying

SALAD
4 good quality anchovies
2 tablespoons extra virgin olive oil
juice of 1 lemon
1 radicchio head, outer leaves discarded
10 pea sprouts
handful of good quality capers, rinsed well

1. To make the fritters place the mozzarella, lemon zest, parsley, fennel seeds, and breadcrumbs in a large bowl and mix well. Sift flour and baking powder directly into the bowl then add the milk, beaten egg, salt, and pepper. Mix gently but thoroughly to combine all ingredients into a batter.

2. Heat a frying pan with enough grapeseed oil to coat the bottom but ensuring the fritters aren't swimming in oil.

3. Spoon a large tablespoonful of batter at a time into the pan. I recommend you cook no more than three fritters at once to ensure you don't crowd the pan and thus slow down the cooking process. Cook on medium–high heat for 2 minutes on each side. Once they have browned, set fritters on a plate and cover with aluminum foil so they stay warm while the others are cooking.

4. To assemble the salad, roughly chop the anchovies and mix with the olive oil and lemon juice.

5. Arrange the radicchio, pea sprouts, and capers on a platter.

6. To serve, place the fritters onto the salad and pour over the anchovy olive oil and sprinkle over the extra parsley leaves. Serve immediately.

North African Sunshine Chicken

Serves 4

Oranges are like pure sunshine, and cardamom and orange have a special affinity. This chicken dish will be a sure hit with mid-week guests. Marinate the chicken the night before to make this a really fast meal. It can also be cooked on the barbecue.

MARINADE
18 cardamom pods, crushed to remove seeds
4 cloves garlic, peeled
1 tablespoon salt
1 teaspoon black peppercorns
1 mace blade
2 teaspoons ground cinnamon
finely grated zest and juice of 2 oranges

4 free-range chicken thighs
grapeseed oil for frying
2 tablespoons orange blossom water

1. Using a mortar and pestle, grind the cardamom seeds with the garlic, salt, peppercorns, mace, and cinnamon. Add a little orange juice to make a paste, then transfer to a bowl and add the rest of the juice and zest.

2. Add the chicken to the paste, mixing well and marinate for at least 4 hours or overnight.

3. Preheat the oven to 400°F/200°C. Place an oven safe dish in the oven to heat.

4. Heat a little grapeseed oil in a frying pan until very hot. Sear the chicken thighs for about 4 minutes on each side or until they are well browned.

5. Transfer the chicken to the hot dish and bake in the oven for 15–20 minutes or until the juices run clear when a knife is inserted close to the joint. Remove from the oven and allow to rest for 3–5 minutes to cool to an easy eating temperature. Pour the orange blossom water over the chicken and serve with a simple salad.

Chicken in a Couscous Coat

Serves 2

This super-fast-to-cook dish is ideal for those nights when you get home late after a hard day at work. The combination of fresh and healthy ingredients will leave you feeling light after your meal rather than stuffed and uncomfortable.

COATING

½ cup couscous
1 teaspoon Hungarian paprika
2 teaspoons whole cumin seeds, toasted and ground
2 teaspoons whole coriander seeds, toasted and ground
1 teaspoon salt
½ teaspoon freshly ground black pepper
3 tablespoons cilantro, finely chopped
grated zest and juice of 1 lemon
freshly boiled water

CHICKEN

6 tablespoons all-purpose flour
2 single chicken breasts, skin and any fat removed, washed and patted dry
2 eggs, beaten
grapeseed oil for frying

SALAD

2 cups salad greens or an assortment of seasonal vegetables, e.g. fresh blanched beans and asparagus
¼ cup extra virgin olive oil
juice of 1 lemon
¼ teaspoon sea salt
¼ teaspoon freshly ground black pepper

1. Preheat oven to 350°F/180°C. Combine the dry coating ingredients in a shallow bowl and mix well. Add the cilantro, lemon zest and juice, and enough hot water to cover the couscous by ¾ inch. Cover with plastic wrap and set aside until the grains have absorbed all the liquid.

2. Sprinkle the flour on a plate. Dip the chicken first in the flour, then in the beaten egg, and lastly roll them in the couscous to coat.

3. Heat the grapeseed oil in a frying pan over medium heat. Sear each breast for about 3 minutes on each side, then put them into the oven for 12–15 minutes until completely cooked through. Lift out and drain on paper towels.

4. Serve with a salad of fresh greens and any other in-season vegetable, simply dressed with some extra virgin olive oil and lemon juice, a little sea salt and pepper.

Young Ginger with Shrimp

Serves 2–4

For the short time that fresh young ginger is available, make the most of it. Much more delicate and fragrant in flavor than the grown-up stuff, young ginger can even be eaten raw. Make this dish with peeled or unpeeled shrimp – it's up to you.

  1 tablespoon fish sauce
  2½-inch piece tender ginger root, grated
  4 shallots, peeled and roughly chopped
  4 cloves garlic, peeled and finely chopped
  ¾-inch piece fresh turmeric, grated
  3 tablespoons Hungarian paprika
  5 tablespoons grapeseed oil
  20 large raw shrimp
  6 tomatoes, roughly chopped
  8 kaffir lime leaves, spines removed and finely sliced, plus extra for garnish
  1 teaspoon salt
  1 teaspoon sugar
  2 spring onions, finely sliced
  steamed white rice to serve

1. Using a mortar and pestle, grind together the fish sauce, ginger, shallots, garlic, and turmeric to form a paste. Add the paprika and mix in.

2. Heat 1 tablespoon of the oil in a wok. Fry the paste until it is beginning to brown and the oil is beginning to seep out. Add the shrimp and stir-fry for 1–2 minutes until partially cooked and changing in color to pink, then remove from the wok and set aside.

3. Add the tomatoes, kaffir lime leaves, salt, and sugar to the wok and cook over medium–high heat until it starts to bubble. Cook, uncovered, for 10 minutes to reduce. Add a little water if it starts to look too dry and sticks. The end result should be quite a dry paste.

4. Add the shrimp to finish cooking them through, along with any liquid that has accumulated, and heat for 2–3 minutes. Add the spring onions and mix through.

5. Garnish with fresh, finely chopped kaffir lime leaves and serve with bowls of steamed rice.

✤ Couldn't-be-simpler Summer Salad

Serves 6

Fava beans have a fresh, crisp flavor and attractive bright green color. By all means use fresh fava beans and peas if available, but frozen also work well. Once defrosted, they don't need cooking.

SALAD
1 x 14 oz can cannellini beans, well rinsed and drained
8 cherry tomatoes, washed and halved
1 small red onion, peeled and finely sliced
1 large bunch Italian (flat-leaf) parsley
14 oz frozen fava beans, defrosted and skins removed
7 oz frozen peas, defrosted

DRESSING
2 teaspoons ground sumac
2 teaspoons toasted cumin seeds
2 cloves garlic, peeled and finely chopped
½ cup olive oil
1 teaspoon salt
½ teaspoon freshly ground black pepper

1. Mix all the salad ingredients together well then gently place them in a large, flat serving bowl.

2. Place the dressing ingredients in a small bowl and whisk to combine. Alternatively, place them in a screw-top jar and shake to combine.

3. Pour the dressing over the salad and leave to infuse for 10 minutes prior to serving. For a simple lunch add some good quality canned tuna, barbecued fish, or poultry.

✤ Spiced Squash

Serves 4 with other accompaniments

This is a fast mid-week number that you can throw in the oven and leave to do its own thing. Serve with toasted pita bread, yogurt with mint leaves, chunks of cucumber, and a hearty grain, such as barley or red rice, for extra texture.

2 lb butternut or kabocha squash, peeled and cut into bite-sized pieces
10 shallots, peeled and halved if they are larger than ¾ inch
4 tablespoons grapeseed oil
¾-inch piece ginger root, peeled and julienned
4 teaspoons cumin seeds
4 tablespoons coriander seeds
2 mild red chilies, such as Anaheim, seeded and finely sliced
1 tablespoon sugar

1. Preheat the oven to 375°F/190°C.

2. Combine all the ingredients in a roasting dish and mix so that the vegetables are coated with the oil and seeds. Bake for 25 minutes.

3. Serve immediately.

✣ Pirate Chicken

Serves 4

Jerked chicken is said to have originated from the Caribbean where the spread of spices was partially due to pirates plundering vessels and selling the goods at ports around the area. A heady spice mix, this jerk paste can also be used for fish, shrimp, and pork.

JERK PASTE
¼ cup toasted allspice berries
1 toasted cinnamon stick
3 habañero chilies, seeded and finely chopped
1 small red onion, peeled and roughly chopped
6 spring onions, roughly chopped
¼ nutmeg, freshly grated
1 bunch thyme, leaves picked off and stalks discarded
1 teaspoon sea salt
¼ cup grapeseed oil
4 organic chicken marylands (thigh and leg joined)

SALAD
2 avocados, peeled and flesh roughly chopped
½ pint cherry tomatoes, roughly chopped
3 sprigs chopped fresh mint
2 sprigs chopped fresh cilantro
2 teaspoons red wine vinegar
3 tablespoons extra virgin olive oil
juice of 1 lime

2 chapati breads per person

1. To make the paste, grind the toasted spices to a fine powder. Transfer to a food processor and add the chili, onion, spring onion, nutmeg, and thyme and process until a paste is formed.

2. Place in a large bowl and stir through the salt and oil. Add the chicken and massage into the skin. Marinate in the refrigerator for as long as possible (preferably overnight).

3. Preheat the oven to 425°F/220°C or heat the barbecue.

4. Bring the chicken back to room temperature and cook for 12–15 minutes on each side or until the juices run clear when pricked in the thickest part with a sharp knife or skewer.

5. Combine the salad ingredients and set aside for 30 minutes for the flavors to infuse. Arrange the chicken, salad, and bread on a large platter for all to share.

Portable Feasts

Spicy street food is a part of almost every culture's cuisine. No silverware is required – just fingers – so the key to preparing this kind of food is simplicity. It is all about knockout flavors and the convenience of eating away from home, whether it's a workday packed lunch or a picnic at the beach.

❧ Vietnamese Baguettes

Serves 4

Imagine Vietnamese-flavored meatloaf sliced and adorned with a tangy dressing then stuffed into a baguette. Alternatively, try lightly frying triangles of the meatloaf and serving as finger food, with the dressing as a dipping sauce, or on top of soupy noodles.

MEATLOAF
1 lb ground pork
2 tablespoons fish sauce
2 teaspoons ground cinnamon
2 teaspoons sugar
1 teaspoon freshly ground black pepper
1 tablespoon arrowroot or cornstarch
4 shallots, peeled and finely chopped
3 cloves garlic, peeled and finely chopped
1 red serrano chili, seeded and finely chopped
2 kaffir lime leaves, spines removed, finely chopped
1 spring onion, finely chopped
1 tablespoon light soy sauce
1 teaspoon salt

DRESSING
1 Thai red chili, finely chopped
1 teaspoon *nam prik pao*
1 teaspoon sesame oil
1 teaspoon fish sauce
1 teaspoon light Chinese soy sauce
4 tablespoons grapeseed oil

1 baguette, cut into 4 pieces
1 avocado
½ cup mung beans
½ iceberg lettuce
½ English cucumber, finely sliced
½ cup cilantro leaves

1. Preheat the oven to 325°F/160°C.

2. Combine the ground pork with the rest of the meatloaf ingredients in a large bowl. Mix well to ensure that everything is well combined and evenly distributed. If time allows, set aside for 2 hours for the flavors to infuse, but this is not essential.

3. Press the mixture into a greased oblong terrine or loaf pan, approximately 12 x 8 inches, and cover with aluminum foil.

4. Place the loaf pan in a larger baking dish and pour water around the smaller dish to come half-way up its sides.

5. Bake for 50 minutes, then uncover and lift out of the larger dish. Return to the oven and bake for 15–20 minutes until the top is crisp and brown. Remove from the oven and cool before turning out.

6. To make the dressing, combine all ingredients in a jar with a screw-top lid. Shake well to ensure that it is well mixed.

7. Thinly slice the meatloaf and stuff into baguette quarters with avocado, mung bean sprouts, lettuce, cucumber slices, cilantro leaves, and the dressing.

Armenian Street Bread

Makes 8 large or 16 small pizza-like rounds

A cross between pizza and flatbread, this street snack is full of spicy flavor.

DOUGH
3 tablespoons active dry yeast
1¼ cups warm water
1 teaspoon sugar
3¾ cups white bread flour
1 teaspoon salt
2 tablespoons olive oil

FILLING
2 tablespoons grapeseed oil
2 white onions, peeled and finely chopped
4 cloves garlic, peeled and finely chopped
1 lb ground lamb
2 tomatoes, skinned and finely chopped
2 teaspoons salt
1 teaspoon sugar
juice of 1 lemon
2 teaspoons tomato paste
6 tablespoons finely chopped Italian (flat-leaf) parsley
9 oz ricotta cheese mixed with 1 tablespoon olive oil to make a smooth paste
2 teaspoons toasted cumin seeds
1 teaspoon chili flakes

TOPPING
2 tablespoons ground sumac
juice of 1 lemon
6 tablespoons finely chopped Italian (flat-leaf) parsley

1. To make the dough, combine the yeast with ½ cup of warm water in a medium-sized bowl. Add the sugar, then leave to froth for 5 minutes. Add the other ingredients and mix well. Turn out onto a floured surface and knead for 10 minutes until the dough is smooth and elastic. Transfer to a clean, well-greased bowl and cover with plastic wrap. Place in a warm spot and leave to rise for 2 hours.

2. Preheat the oven to 465°F/240°C.

3. To make the filling, heat the oil in a frying pan and cook the onion and garlic for 3 minutes until soft. Add the lamb and brown slightly. Add the tomatoes, salt, sugar, lemon juice, and tomato paste and cook, uncovered, for 10–15 minutes until reduced slightly. Remove from the heat and allow to cool before stirring through the parsley. Drain off any excess liquid that may have formed and set aside.

4. When the dough has risen, knead it again then divide into 8 balls or 16 smaller balls. Roll out each ball as thin as possible and transfer the bases to greased preheated oven trays (or, better still, a hot pizza stone). Top each with a layer of lamb and some ricotta then sprinkle over the cumin seeds and chili flakes.

5. Bake in batches for 8–10 minutes, depending on the thickness and size of the flatbreads, until the tops are brown and the edges are crispy but they remain soft enough to roll.

6. Sprinkle the cooked flatbreads with sumac and parsley and squeeze some lemon juice over them. Roll up, rolling the sides in on themselves and eat immediately or leave flat and eat like a pizza.

NOTE: When cooking in batches, the temperature of the oven will drop between taking the breads out and putting the next batch in so it's important to bring the temperature back to 465°F/240°C each time.

The Spice Kitchen

Caraway Onion Cheese Scones

Makes 8–9 large scones

Scones are quick and easy to make and spices can transform the average scone into a really tasty morning snack. For variations, add anything you might have on hand, such as leftover roasted vegetables, ham, or bacon.

2 red onions, peeled and finely sliced
2 teaspoons fennel seeds
4 teaspoons caraway seeds
2 tablespoons olive oil
5 teaspoons baking powder
4 cups all-purpose flour
2 teaspoons salt
4 tablespoons cold butter
1 egg, beaten
4 tablespoons plain yogurt
2 cups finely grated pecorino cheese
½ cup milk plus a little extra
sea salt and freshly ground black pepper

1. Preheat the oven to 375°F/190°C.

2. Place the onions in an oven dish with half the fennel and caraway seeds and the olive oil and mix well. Bake for 15–20 minutes or until the onion is brown and soft. Set aside until required but leave the oven on.

3. Sift the dry ingredients together in a large bowl, then grate in the butter. Using your fingertips, rub the butter into the flour until it resembles breadcrumbs.

4. Using a mortar and pestle or spice grinder, grind together the remaining fennel and caraway seeds and add them to the butter and flour mix. Add the beaten egg, yogurt, and half the cheese. Mix in half a cup of milk and knead well, adding a little more flour if necessary.

5. Tip out onto a well-floured surface and knead for a bit to make sure everything is well mixed and the texture is nice and smooth. This usually takes about 5 minutes. Roll out to about ¾ inch thick, then cut the dough in half. Roll out each piece again so that both are long and thin.

6. Spread one piece with the roasted onion and seed mix and the remaining half of the cheese. Place the other piece of dough on top and push it down all around to seal the sides. Brush a little milk over the top layer and sprinkle with sea salt and pepper. Cut into squares and place on a greased oven tray.

7. Bake for 10–12 minutes or until golden brown.

8. Serve with butter while hot.

🦁 Lebanese Wings

Serves 4

Tahini is the main ingredient in this great barbecue recipe. Here it is used as a binder in a marinade. Use this recipe for any chicken cut, firm-fleshed fish, or pork.

MARINADE
8 tablespoons tahini
juice of 2 lemons
1 teaspoon Spanish smoked sweet paprika
4 teaspoons whole cumin seeds, toasted and finely ground
4 cloves garlic, peeled and finely chopped
3 tablespoons grapeseed oil
1 teaspoon sea salt
1 teaspoon freshly ground black pepper

16 chicken wings, well washed
chopped Italian (flat-leaf) parsley and lemon wedges to garnish

1. Combine all the marinade ingredients in a large bowl and mix well. Add the chicken wings and marinate for 1 hour – or more if time allows.

2. Cook for 10–12 minutes on the barbecue until slightly charred or in an oven preheated to 400°F/200°C (the tahini will release a lot of oil which should be poured off at least once during cooking in order for the wings to turn crispy).

3. Serve hot, garnished with parsley and lemon wedges, as part of a mezze, for lunch, a picnic or as finger food.

🦁 Pilgrims' Eggs

Makes enough for 3–4 to share

A hard-boiled egg has long been an enjoyable picnic staple. Not satisfied with the plain version, however, Muslim pilgrims traditionally used spices to flavor or color their eggs, often frying them in spices.

1 teaspoon salt
¼ teaspoon freshly ground black pepper
2 teaspoons whole cumin seeds, toasted and finely ground
2 teaspoons whole coriander seeds, toasted and finely ground
½ teaspoon ground cinnamon
6 hard-boiled eggs, shelled and halved
grapeseed oil for frying

1. Mix the salt, pepper, and spices together.

2. Heat a little oil in a frying pan and add the eggs, shaking the pan to evenly coat the eggs in oil. Add the spices to the pan and shake again.

3. Serve cold or warm as part of a pilgrim's mezze. Alternatively, serve with salad greens or add to a salad of fried potatoes mixed with a little olive oil and lemon juice.

✵ *Spicy Rolled Indian Omelets*

Serves 1 anytime of the day or night

You can't get much simpler and tastier than a well-made omelet. I like this rolled up in a fresh chapati with Patient Date and Lemon Chutney (page 178) and a few salad leaves for lunch or teamed up with some fresh vegetables for an evening meal.

> 1 tablespoon butter
> 2 free-range eggs
> ½ small onion, peeled and finely chopped
> ½ Thai green chili, halved, seeded, then finely chopped
> 1 tablespoon finely chopped fresh cilantro leaves
> ½ teaspoon sea salt
> ¼ teaspoon freshly ground black pepper
> 1 teaspoon toasted cumin seeds
> 1 teaspoon whole coriander seeds, toasted and finely ground
>
> 1 chapati or roti

1. Heat a frying pan and melt the butter.
2. Beat the eggs and add the rest of the ingredients, beating well.
3. Add the egg mixture to the pan, tilting it so that the vegetables and egg are evenly distributed. Cook until the top is just set, then turn to cook the other side for 1 minute before turning out onto a plate and rolling up in a chapati or roti. Even stuffing into a pita bread will do the trick if you can't find roti or chapati.

Asian Feasting

While any of the following dishes make a wonderfully tasty main meal, a combination of dishes results in an unforgettable feasting experience. Be mindful, however, of how flavor, texture, and color work together when planning a menu.

Some dishes require advance preparation and you'll need to take this into account when you want to serve a combination of dishes so that they are all ready at the same time.

🦁 Summer Fennel Seed and Fish Lettuce Wraps

Serves 4-6

Fennel is teamed here with galangal, but use fresh ginger root if galangal is not available. This fresh, zesty dish is perfect for hot summer evenings. Use chicken instead of fish if you prefer.

½ teaspoon salt
1 lb firm white fish filets
4 thin slices ginger root
2 tablespoons grapeseed oil
3 sticks lemongrass, trimmed and finely sliced
2 teaspoons fennel seeds, toasted
4 cloves garlic, peeled and finely chopped
4 shallots, peeled and finely chopped
4 kaffir lime leaves, spines removed, finely sliced
1 tablespoon fish sauce
juice of 2 limes
1 Anaheim chili, seeded and finely sliced
2 teaspoons sugar
4 tablespoons finely chopped fresh cilantro leaves
1 English cucumber, peeled and seeded then cut into 2 x ½-inch strips
1 spring onion, green part only, sliced lengthwise
2 tablespoons peanuts, toasted and roughly chopped
1 iceberg lettuce, leaves carefully removed so they stay whole

1. Rub the salt into the fish. Transfer to a heatproof bowl that will fit into a large saucepan. Quarter-fill the saucepan with cold water and place the bowl inside. Place the sliced ginger on top of the fish and cover the saucepan with a lid.

2. Bring the water in the saucepan to a boil, then reduce it to a simmer and steam the fish for 10–12 minutes, depending on the thickness of the filets.

3. Remove the pan from the heat, uncover and allow the fish to cool.

4. Heat the oil in a frying pan and fry the lemongrass and fennel seeds until the lemongrass has softened and is beginning to brown. Remove the lemongrass from the pan and drain on paper towels.

5. Reheat the remaining oil in the pan and fry the garlic and shallots until both are crispy.

6. Remove from the pan and drain. Set aside until required.

7. Combine the remaining ingredients except the lettuce in a large bowl. Flake the cooked fish into the bowl and mix well. If time allows, set aside for several hours to allow the flavors to infuse.

8. Encourage diners to serve themselves by spooning some fish mixture into a lettuce leaf and then rolling it up to encase the filling (much like a spring roll).

NOTE: This dish is good served with other complementary finger foods, such as Rolled Sesame Balls (page 145) and Thai Super Snacks (page 60).

Indonesian Pork and Shrimp Balls in Kaffir Lime and Vermicelli Soup

Serves 4-6

Indonesian cuisine draws from a range of influences including Chinese, Indian, Dutch, Portuguese, Spanish, and Arabian. This recipe, best made a day ahead so the flavors develop, is very versatile – any meat or fish can be used.

PORK AND SHRIMP BALLS

9 oz raw shrimp, peeled and finely chopped
9 oz fatty ground pork
1½-inch piece ginger root, peeled and finely chopped
2 medium–hot fresh red chilies, seeded and finely chopped
2 spring onions, halved lengthwis then finely chopped
2 teaspoons well washed and finely chopped cilantro roots
2 tablespoons finely chopped fresh cilantro leaves
3 teaspoons fish sauce
juice of 2 limes
6–8 water chestnuts, finely diced (use canned if fresh are unavailable)
3 tablespoons light soy sauce
1 teaspoon cornstarch or arrowroot
vegetable oil for frying

SOUP

6 cups water
3 chicken carcasses, well washed
2 sticks lemongrass, smashed at the root and the tops trimmed down to fit into the pot
1½-inch piece ginger root
3 kaffir lime leaves, washed
2 cloves garlic, peeled
4–5 cilantro roots, well washed
salt to taste

10½ oz vermicelli or flat rice noodles
1 bunch watercress or baby spinach leaves, well washed and drained
chopped fresh cilantro, finely sliced kaffir lime leaves, and red chili to garnish

1. To make the balls, combine all the ingredients except the oil in a large bowl and mix well. Form into walnut-sized balls and place in a single layer on a large plate. Chill for 10–15 minutes.

2. Heat the oil in a large frying pan and shallow-fry the balls in batches until golden brown. Drain on paper towels and set aside until ready to serve.

3. To make the soup, combine all the ingredients in a large stockpot. Cover and place over low–medium heat until gently simmering and cook for 40 minutes.

4. Strain the soup through a sieve and keep warm. Taste to check seasoning and adjust accordingly. Remove carcasses. At this stage, you can pick the meat from the carcasses and include it in the soup if you wish.

5. Soak the noodles in warm water for 5 minutes if using vermicelli or cook for 4–5 minutes if using dried flat noodles, then drain well. Divide the noodles and prepared balls between the required number of bowls, then ladle in the soup. Garnish with the cilantro, lime leaves, and chili. Serve immediately.

Indonesian Chicken Rempah

Serves 4

The ingredients in rempah, a spice mix used throughout Indonesia, can vary, though turmeric is fairly standard. Look out for green peppercorns attached to their vines and soaked in brine and wash them well before using.

CHICKEN
2 lb chicken pieces, cut into 1½ x 1½-inch chunks but left on bone
2 teaspoons salt
2 teaspoons brined green peppercorns, finely chopped
vegetable oil for frying

REMPAH SPICE MIX
8 candle nuts or macadamia nuts
8 small shallots, peeled and finely chopped
5 cloves garlic, peeled and chopped
1½-inch piece turmeric root, peeled and grated or 1 teaspoon ground turmeric
1½-inch piece galangal root, peeled and grated
1 tablespoon finely chopped fresh cilantro leaves
2 teaspoons shrimp paste

SAUCE
2 sticks lemongrass
1 x 14 oz can coconut milk
juice of 1 lime
5 kaffir lime leaves, washed
1 lb 2 oz pumpkin, peeled and cut into 1½-inch chunks

6 tablespoons shredded, unsweetened coconut, toasted
1 banana, peeled and finely sliced
10 candle or macadamia nuts, toasted then broken up

1. Season the chicken pieces with the salt and peppercorns. Heat the oil in a large frying pan and fry the chicken until browned. Transfer to a deep heavy-based saucepan and set aside.

2. To make the spice mix, crush the nuts in a food processor or in a mortar and pestle until they are well broken down and are fine in texture. Add the shallots and garlic and process or grind to mix. Add the remaining ingredients and mix well.

3. Heat a little more oil in the pan used to fry the chicken and add the spice mix. Cook for 2 minutes, then drain off any excess oil. Sprinkle the spice mix over the chicken.

4. Make the sauce. Remove the outer layers from the lemongrass. Smash the root ends, then trim the tops to fit the saucepan. Add with the rest of the ingredients to the chicken in the saucepan. Add enough water to just cover the chicken and mix well. Simmer over low heat for 45 minutes, then increase the heat and cook for a further 10–15 minutes or until the coconut milk has reduced to a thick consistency that holds the curry together.

5. Serve the curry topped with the coconut, banana, and nuts with plain steamed white rice.

NOTE: If chicken bones are a problem for any reason, allow the cooked chicken pieces to cool, then remove the bones before returning the meat to the sauce. Watch cooking time as chicken can become stringy if overcooked.

🦁 Siamese Mussaman Chicken Curry

Serves 4-6

Best made several days ahead for maximum flavor, this curry – adapted from a recipe devised by master of Thai cooking David Thompson – involves quite a lot of preparation but is well worth the effort.

MUSSAMAN CURRY PASTE

2 tablespoons grapeseed oil
5 bird's-eye chilies, seeded, soaked in warm water for 20 minutes then drained
4 shallots, peeled and cut into quarters
6 cloves garlic, peeled
¾-inch piece fresh galangal, peeled and sliced
2 sticks lemongrass, trimmed and root ends bashed
1 bunch cilantro, trimmed down to roots, well washed and roughly chopped
1 tablespoon coriander seeds, toasted and finely ground
2 teaspoons cumin seeds, toasted and finely ground
5 cloves, toasted and finely ground
2 mace blades, toasted and finely ground
½ nutmeg, freshly grated
¾-inch piece cassia, toasted and finely ground
seeds from a brown cardamom, finely ground
1 teaspoon salt
2 tablespoons peanuts, toasted and ground

CURRY

1 free-range chicken
4 tablespoons grapeseed oil
4 medium potatoes, peeled and chopped into 1¼-inch cubes
2 brown onions, peeled and finely chopped
6 shallots, peeled and finely chopped
6 cups coconut milk
2 bay leaves
½ cup peanuts, toasted and ground to a smooth consistency
4 tablespoons fish sauce
2 tablespoons grated palm sugar
4 tablespoons tamarind water (achieved by soaking 8 tablespoons tamarind paste in 5 tablespoons of hot water, then passing it through a sieve)
1 cup pineapple juice
toasted peanuts to garnish

1. Make the curry paste first. Heat the oil in a wok and add the chilies, shallots, garlic, galangal, lemongrass, and cilantro. Fry until fragrant. Allow to cool, then process to a paste in a mortar and pestle or blender. Transfer to a bowl and set aside.

2. Next, grind the seeds, cloves, mace blades, nutmeg, cassia, and cardamon to a fine texture. Combine with the salt and peanuts. Add to the fried ingredients and mix well. Set aside.

3. Wash the chicken, inside and out, and trim off all excess fat. Cut into serving-sized pieces.

4. Heat the oil in a wok and brown the chicken pieces. Transfer to a plate or bowl lined with paper towels and set aside while you brown the potato, onion, and shallot. Drain the vegetables on some clean paper towels and set aside.

5. Drain any remaining oil from the wok. Return the chicken pieces to the wok and pour in enough coconut milk to just cover the pieces (you should have some left over). Add the bay leaves, ground peanuts, and fish sauce and simmer over low heat for 10 minutes.

6. Add the cooked vegetables and simmer for a further 15 minutes.

7. Meanwhile, heat the remaining coconut milk in a saucepan. Add the curry paste and simmer over low heat for 10–15 minutes. Stir occasionally to prevent sticking or burning (as the mixture reduces it will start to splutter). When it has reduced to an oily paste, add the palm sugar and tamarind water. Taste and add more sugar or tamarind water if required.

8. Add the chicken and potato to the saucepan and stir in the pineapple juice. Taste to check seasoning and adjust accordingly.

9. Serve with steamed white rice and garnish with the toasted peanuts.

🌸 Unripe Salad

Serves 3–4 as part of a combination of dishes

Served as part of a multi-course meal, this sweet and sour dish will cleanse the palate and aid digestion. If green papaya is unavailable, use an unripe mango or just the cucumber.

 2 bird's-eye chilies, finely chopped
 juice of 2 limes
 3 whole cloves, toasted
 1 tablespoon fish sauce
 1 tablespoon grated palm sugar
 1⅔ green (unripe) papaya, peeled and grated or shredded using a mandoline
 handful beansprouts, well washed
 1 small cucumber, peeled, seeded and grated finely using a mandoline
 3 tablespoons mirin or Chinese white vinegar

1. Crush the chilies with the next four ingredients in a mortar and pestle. Add about ½ cup of the shredded papaya and crush into the mixture.

2. Tip into a bowl and add the remaining ingredients, including the rest of the shredded papaya, mixing well.

3. Allow to stand for 30 minutes before serving.

🦎 *Thai Super Snacks*

Serves 4–6 as finger food

Street food is what Asian cuisine is all about. Deliciously tempting and very portable, these snacks are immediately satisfying and work well either as finger food or part of an Asian feast.

1 stem green peppercorns in brine, well rinsed
14 oz organic chicken thigh meat, boneless
3½ oz free-range ground pork
2 sticks lemongrass, ends trimmed, outer hard leaves discarded, finely chopped
3 cloves garlic, peeled and roughly chopped
1¼-inch piece ginger root, roughly chopped
3 kaffir lime leaves, spines removed, finely chopped
juice and zest of 1 lime
3 shallots, peeled and roughly chopped
3 tablespoons roughly chopped Vietnamese mint
1 tablespoon roughly chopped mint
1 spring onion, roughly chopped
½ cup coconut cream
2 tablespoons cornstarch
2 tablespoons fish sauce
1 tablespoon Chinese light soy sauce
grapeseed oil for deep-frying

DIPPING SAUCE
3 tablespoons Chinese white vinegar
1 teaspoon sesame oil
1 clove crushed garlic
½ teaspoon sesame seeds
1 mild red chili, seeded and very finely sliced

1. Remove the peppercorns from the stem. Place in a food processor or blender with the rest of the ingredients and process to form a thick paste. Leaving the paste in the processor bowl, transfer to the refrigerator and chill for 2 hours.

2. Form the mixture into bite-sized oval or sausage shapes. Chill for another hour.

3. Heat a generous quantity of oil in a large saucepan until almost smoking. Drop the shapes, a few at a time, into the hot oil in batches. Remove once they are brown (test one to check it is cooked through) and drain on paper towels. Serve immediately with dipping sauce.

4. To make the dipping sauce, combine ingredients together in a bowl.

Vietnamese Perfumed Fish

Serves 3 as a main dish or 6 as part of a combination of dishes

This unique take on a classic dish is rich in color and flavor. You can make it into a noodle or rice dish if you like or serve as part of a banquet. It is important to use young feathery dill that is not too woody in texture.

VIETNAMESE CHILLI PASTE
1 stem green peppercorns in brine, well rinsed
4 cloves garlic, peeled
1½-inch piece ginger root, roughly chopped
1½-inch piece fresh turmeric, grated
2 teaspoons caraway seeds, toasted
2 tablespoons fish sauce
2 mild red chilies, seeded and finely chopped
juice and zest of 1 lime
1 teaspoon salt
½ teaspoon freshly ground black pepper
1 teaspoon sugar

FISH
1 lb firm-fleshed white fish filets, e.g. ling, gurnard, or tarakihi
2 tablespoons grapeseed oil
1 big bunch dill, roughly chopped
3 tablespoons water
5 tablespoons toasted and crushed peanuts

1. To make the chili paste, remove the peppercorns from the stem. Place in a mortar and pestle with the garlic, ginger, turmeric, and caraway seeds and grind together to form a paste. Mix together the fish sauce, chilies, lime juice and zest, salt, pepper, and sugar and add to the paste.

2. Place the fish filets in a shallow dish. You have the option of cutting them into smaller pieces which will cook faster or leaving them whole. Small pieces would be more suited to a banquet meal. Coat the fish filets with the paste and marinate for at least 30 minutes, but preferably 2 hours.

3. Heat the oil in a large frying pan until hot and add the fish. Don't mix it about too much or it will begin to break up. Cook until brown underneath, then carefully turn each piece over to brown the other side.

4. Sprinkle the dill on top of the fish and add the water to the pan. Cover and cook for 3–4 minutes until the fish is cooked through.

5. Scatter the peanuts over the fish and carefully mix through with the dill. Serve immediately.

🦁 Vietnamese Dinner Noodles

Serves 4

Although there appears to be lots of ingredients in this dish, it is relatively easy to make – ideal for those nights when you want maximum taste without too much effort.

6 dried shitake mushrooms
7 oz frozen shrimp, defrosted with tails and heads removed and roughly diced
1 cinnamon stick
3 star anise
2 teaspoons sugar
2 teaspoons salt
2 eggs, beaten
3 teaspoons grapeseed oil
1½-inch piece ginger root, peeled and julienned
6 cloves garlic, peeled
5 oz ground pork
1 stick lemongrass, trimmed and finely chopped
9 oz fresh soft or dried flat rice noodles
6 fresh or canned water chestnuts, diced
2 spring onions, finely chopped
1 teaspoon fish sauce
5 teaspoons light soy sauce
3 teaspoons finely chopped fresh cilantro leaves
3 teaspoons finely chopped fresh mint leaves
2 teaspoons finely chopped Vietnamese mint
handful mung bean sprouts
Vietnamese mint, star anise, and lemon wedges to garnish

1. Soak the mushrooms, shrimp, cinnamon, and star anise in enough warm water to just cover them and allow to infuse for at least 30 minutes, but ideally overnight.

2. Add half the sugar and salt to the beaten egg and mix well.

3. Heat 1 teaspoon of the grapeseed oil in a wok over high heat. Pour the egg mixture into the wok and roll the wok from side to side so the egg distributes evenly to form a good-sized omelet. Once the underside is golden brown, flip the omelet over for a few seconds. Remove from the wok and set aside to cool.

4. Heat the rest of the oil in the wok and cook the ginger and garlic for 1–2 minutes. Once the garlic starts to brown, add the ground pork and lemongrass and mix well, loosening it with a fork to stop it clumping. Stir-fry until the pork has browned evenly, then remove from the wok and set aside.

5. Reserving the soaking water, remove the mushrooms and shrimp and roughly chop. Remove and discard the spices from the water.

6. If using fresh noodles soak them in warm water until softened. If using dried, cook to package instructions. Drain and set aside.

7. Heat the wok once more and, once it is very hot, add the browned pork. Add the water chestnuts, mushrooms, shrimp, and spring onion. Stir-fry for a couple of minutes until the pork begins to stick a little, then add the reserved soaking water, fish sauce, remaining salt and sugar, and soy sauce. Layer the chopped herbs and bean sprouts on top of the mix and then work it all in together.

8. Once the vegetables and herbs have just wilted, add the noodles, mixing well, then distribute between the bowls. Garnish with Vietnamese mint, star anise, and lemon wedges for squeezing overtop.

Luxury Sundays

Sundays are the ideal time for cooking a big paella, firing up the barbecue, or making a delicious tapas selection to share with family and friends. The combination of good friendships, good food, and the realization that work shouldn't rule our lives leaves me with a warm glow.

Many of the dishes in this chapter can be prepared and left to cook slowly in the oven while you have a catnap, do some gardening, or sit and chat with friends.

✥ Lovers' Oxtail Stew

Serves 4–5

A traditional Yemeni blend, hawayji is fiery but fragrant and a great addition to soups and stews. Caraway is said to encourage fidelity. Added to this hearty stew, how could your lover even consider venturing elsewhere?

HAWAYJI SPICE MIX
6 teaspoons finely ground black pepper
3 teaspoons toasted caraway seeds
20 cardamom pods, crushed, seeds removed and toasted
2 teaspoons ground turmeric

STEW
2 lb oxtail
6 tablespoons all-purpose flour
2 teaspoons salt
1 teaspoon freshly ground black pepper
4 tablespoons butter
2 teaspoons hawayji spice mix
3 large red onions, peeled and roughly chopped
6 cloves garlic, peeled and chopped
½ cup yellow dhal lentils
8 cups water
5 tomatoes, skinned and roughly chopped
2 bay leaves
1 orange, cut into eighths with the skin on
grated zest and juice of 1 orange
large bunch spinach, well washed

1. To make the hawayji, combine the ingredients and grind to a fine texture. Store in an airtight jar in a dark, cool place and use within 2 months.

2. To make the stew, preheat the oven to 325°F/160°C.

3. Wash and pat dry the oxtail.

4. Combine the flour with the salt and pepper in a bowl or plastic bag. Toss the oxtail in the seasoned flour to coat.

5. Heat the butter in a large heavy-based oven safe dish and gently brown the oxtail over low heat. Remove the oxtail and add the hawayji, onion, garlic, and lentils. Stir to coat with the butter before adding the water, tomatoes, bay leaves, orange segments, zest and juice.

6. Cover and place in the oven to cook for 3 hours.

7. At the end of the cooking time, check seasoning and adjust accordingly. Remove the meat from the bones if preferred, or serve on the bone.

8. Reduce the remaining liquid if there is too much. Add the spinach and stir through.

9. Serve with plain rice.

NOTE: This dish improves with age. It is best made several days ahead and reheated thoroughly. Take care to avoid burning the lentils.

🦂 Tequila-fueled Blackened Chicken with Red Beans

Serves 4

Real blackened chicken served with robustly spiced and well-cooked beans is comfort food at its best. And while the brown cardamom in this dish isn't traditional, it imparts a great smoky flavor, which is why it is often used in tandoori spice blends.

BLACKENING MIX

2 teaspoons ground ginger
3 cloves garlic, peeled
2 teaspoons freshly chopped oregano
2 teaspoons Spanish sweet smoked paprika
1 teaspoon ground dried chili such as pasilla or chipotle
1 whole brown cardamom, crushed to remove seeds
2 teaspoons whole cumin seeds, toasted and finely ground
2 mace blades, toasted and finely ground

2 tablespoons grapeseed oil
4 free-range or organic chicken thighs (or breast if preferred), skin removed and well washed

RED BEANS

3 dried smoked chipotle chilies
1 lb dried red kidney beans, soaked for 12 hours and refreshed with cold water as often as possible during soaking time
3 tablespoons grapeseed oil
2 red onions, peeled and finely chopped
6 cloves garlic, peeled and finely chopped
2 teaspoons whole coriander seeds, toasted and finely ground
6 large tomatoes, chopped
1 tablespoon tomato paste
1 teaspoon sugar
2 teaspoons salt
1 teaspoon freshly ground black pepper
1 tablespoon red wine vinegar
⅔ cup tequila
juice and finely grated zest of 2 limes
8 tablespoons fresh cilantro leaves, finely chopped
lime wedges to garnish

1. To make the blackening mix, combine all the ingredients except the oil and the chicken and mix well. Just before you are ready to coat the chicken, stir the oil through the mix.

2. Coat the chicken with the blackening mix and allow to marinate for 3 hours in the refrigerator.

3. To prepare the beans, soak the chilies in a little hot water for 20 minutes until softened. Remove the softened chilies and finely slice, reserving the soaking water.

4. Wash and drain the beans, then place in a large saucepan and cover with cold water. Bring to a boil, drain and rinse. Repeat this step until the beans are once more boiling, then reduce the heat and simmer for 40 minutes or until tender. Drain, rinse well and set aside. Remove 1 cup of cooked beans and, either in a mortar and pestle or food processor, crush or pulse them to a rough paste. Set aside and refrigerate. This gives the dish a little more texture.

5. Preheat the oven to 400°F/200°C.

6. In a large heavy-based frying pan heat the oil and cook the onion and garlic until softened. Stir in the coriander seeds and cook for 2 minutes. Add the sliced chilies, tomatoes and tomato paste, sugar, salt and pepper and stir well. Add the reserved chili water and the vinegar. Simmer over low heat for 20 minutes, adding a little water if it starts to look too dry. Add the cooked beans and crushed beans, mix well and simmer for a further 15 minutes.

7. Place a roasting dish in the hot oven.

8. Heat another 2 tablespoons of grapeseed oil in a heavy-based frying pan and sear the chicken, cooking each side for 45 seconds. Add the tequila to the pan and allow it to evaporate before removing the chicken and placing it in the heated roasting dish. Return the dish to the oven and cook for 12–15 minutes or until the juices of the chicken run clear.

9. Just before serving, add the lime juice, zest, and most of the fresh cilantro to the beans (reserving a little to garnish). Adjust seasonings if required.

10. Serve on a large platter with the chicken resting on top, garnished with fresh cilantro and lime wedges, with shot glasses of tequila.

Comfort Baked Eggs with Ricotta

Serves 4

Baked eggs are definitely comfort food. Excellent for a tasty yet easy mid-week dish or for Sunday brunch after a big night out, there is something about them that makes you feel instantly sleepy and ready for bed. Make it in separate ramekins or in one large baking dish.

    2 tablespoons butter
    2 bunches Swiss chard, woody stalks removed, well washed and finely chopped
    3 cloves garlic
    1 white onion, peeled and finely sliced
    1 teaspoon salt
    $\frac{1}{3}$ cup half & half
    $3\frac{1}{2}$ oz ricotta cheese
    $\frac{1}{2}$ nutmeg, freshly grated
    4 eggs
    sea salt and freshly ground black pepper

1. Preheat the oven to 350°F/180°C.

2. Melt the butter in a large saucepan. Add the Swiss chard, garlic, onion, and salt and cook until the vegetables have softened. Drain through a sieve, then squeeze out any excess water.

3. Divide the cooked mixture between four ramekins or one baking dish. Make a well in each ramekin or four wells if using the one dish.

4. Combine the half & half and ricotta in a bowl and beat well. Add most of the nutmeg.

5. Carefully crack the eggs into the prepared wells, then pour in the cream mixture. Sprinkle with the rest of the nutmeg, salt, and pepper.

6. Bake for 20–25 minutes or until the egg is soft.

7. Serve with toasted chunks of bread.

Overleaf (left): Tequila-fueled Blackened Chicken with Red Beans; (right): Chicken Mole Negro (recipe pages 72–3)

Chicken Mole Negro

Choose a bittersweet chocolate with cocoa solids of at least 60 percent and it's worth the effort to find chipotle and pasilla chilies as their unique flavors contribute a special element to this dish. Try online and health food stores if you are struggling. I recommend making the mole negro a day in advance to allow the flavors to develop.

MOLE NEGRO
1 onion, peeled and roughly chopped
2 cloves garlic, peeled and finely chopped
grapeseed oil for frying
4 dried chipotle chilies
4 dried pasilla chilies
2 tablespoons sesame seeds
1 oz raw peanuts or blanched almonds, skinned
1 corn tortilla, torn into ½-inch pieces (wheat will do if that is all you can find)
6 semi-dried soft tomatoes (not sundried or in oil)
6 cloves, toasted and finely ground
12 allspice berries, finely ground
2½ teaspoons ground cinnamon
2 teaspoons ground aniseed
1 ripe plantain, peeled and sliced into pieces ¼ inch thick
2 oz dark chocolate
3 teaspoons salt
½ teaspoon freshly ground black pepper

POACHED CHICKEN
1 x 3 lb free-range chicken
1 onion, peeled and halved
1 bay leaf
5 sprigs thyme
5 cilantro stems
5 parsley stems
1 lime, halved
1 teaspoon salt
½ teaspoon freshly ground black pepper
freshly chopped cilantro leaves and fresh corn tortillas to serve

1. To make the mole, cook the onion and garlic in a little oil over low heat until very soft, then set aside.

2. Heat a separate pan without any oil and scorch the chilies until blackened. Set aside.

3. Toast the sesame seeds for 20–30 seconds or until they begin to brown and set aside. Toast the nuts until brown but not burnt and set aside. Toast the tortilla pieces until charred (this gives the dish a delectable smoky flavor) and set aside.

4. Split the chilies and shake out the seeds. Soak the seeded chilies and the semi-dried tomatoes in half a cup of warm water for 30 minutes until softened, then chop roughly, reserving the soaking water.

5. Blend the chilies and chopped tomatoes with the onion and garlic in a food processor or blender to form a paste, adding a little of the reserved soaking water. Add the toasted seeds and nuts and process again, adding more water as required to form a smooth paste. Set aside.

6. Heat a little oil in a frying pan, and gently cook the cloves, allspice berries, cinnamon, and aniseed with the sliced plantain for 5–6 minutes until the plantain has softened and started to brown. Add 3 tablespoons of water to the pan and stir until it evaporates.

7. Transfer the contents of the pan to the food processor or blender along with the charred tortilla and blend to a smooth paste. Set aside.

8. Heat a little oil in the pan and gently fry the sesame seeds, tomato, and nut paste. Allow it to stick a little and brown but not burn. Add the plantain paste and mix well.

9. Add six ladlefuls of the reserved chicken stock, one at a time, mixing thoroughly between each addition to make a thick paste. Ensure that each ladleful of stock is thoroughly absorbed before adding the next (some serious mixing will be required to get the mixture to combine). Grate in the chocolate, then season to taste. Cook the mole paste you have just created for 1 hour covered on medium–low heat. Stir from time to time as it can begin to stick. Refrigerate until required.

10. Remove the lid after an hour and allow to reduce naturally for a further hour. I highly recommend doing this in stages over a few days. The flavor is greatly enhanced if it is allowed to sit overnight in the refrigerator and cooked again the following day.

11. To poach the chicken, place the chicken and the next eight ingredients in a stockpot with enough water to cover and bring to a boil. Using a slotted spoon, lift off any scum from the surface and discard. Reduce the heat and simmer for 45 minutes. Turn off the heat and leave to stand. When cool enough to handle, remove the chicken from the stock and shred meat, reserving the stock. Refrigerate until required.

12. When ready to serve, return the chicken to the reserved stock and heat through well. If the stock is fresh it can be reserved for another time as it is very fragrant but subtle, but if it has been refrigerated discard it.

13. Heat the mole and spoon into shallow bowls. Top with shredded chicken and cilantro and serve with fresh corn tortillas.

Rioja Red, White, and Green Toasts

Serves 2 for Sunday brunch

Named for the red of the salmon, the white of the wonderfully flavored ham fat, and the green of the fava beans, this tasty brunch dish also works with authentic Spanish chorizo or Italian prosciutto in place of Serrano ham.

> 7 oz frozen fava beans, defrosted and shelled
> 1 teaspoon sherry vinegar
> 6 cloves garlic, roasted in their skins, peeled
> 1 teaspoon Spanish bitter-sweet smoked paprika
> 1 loaf crusty bread, cut into 6 thick slices and toasted
> 2 tablespoons extra virgin olive oil, preferably Spanish
> 6 slices Serrano ham,
> 7 oz piece hot-smoked salmon
> 2 tablespoons Italian (flat-leaf) parsley, chopped

1. Pulse the beans, sherry vinegar, garlic, and paprika in a food processor until chunky but slightly pasty.

2. Rub each slice of bread with a little of the olive oil, then toast.

3. Build a thick layer of fava bean paste on each slice of toast, then top with the ham followed by the flaked salmon. Garnish with the Italian parsley, drizzle over the remaining olive oil and serve.

🦁 Italian Braised Squid

Serves 4

A tasty Italian-inspired dish, this can be served as an entrée, as part of a mezze or even tossed through pasta. It's best served with lots of crusty bread to mop up the juices.

    3 tablespoons olive oil
    1 red onion, peeled and finely chopped
    4 cloves garlic, peeled and finely chopped
    1 leek, halved lengthwise, washed well and cut into half circles ¾ inch wide
    1 fennel bulb, washed well and finely sliced
    2 lb fresh squid, cleaned and innards removed, sliced into pieces
    1 teaspoon sea salt
    ½ teaspoon freshly ground black pepper
    2 teaspoons toasted fennel seeds
    2 teaspoons coriander seeds, toasted and finely ground
    2 medium–hot red chilies, seeded and finely chopped
    grated zest and juice of 2 oranges
    ½ bottle white wine
    4 tablespoons freshly chopped cilantro leaves to garnish

1. Preheat the oven to 300°F/150°C.

2. Heat the olive oil in a frying pan. Sauté the onion and garlic until softened, then add the leek and fennel and cook for 2–3 minutes. Increase the heat and after a minute or so, add the squid, stirring well. Stir in the seasonings, spices, and chili and cook for 3 minutes. Add the orange zest, juice, and white wine. Reduce the heat to a simmer and check seasoning, adjusting if necessary.

3. Transfer the mixture to an oven safe dish and bake for 1 hour.

4. Remove from the oven, lift out the cooked squid and set aside.

5. Transfer the liquid back to the frying pan and reduce over high heat until you have about 6 tablespoons of thickened juice.

6. Return the squid to the liquid and garnish with fresh cilantro leaves. Serve with bread.

NOTE: Fresh squid overwhelms some people. Fair enough – it does look a bit prehistoric. You can get your local fishmonger to clean them up for you, but it's actually pretty simple to manage yourself. Here's how:

1. Slice open the stomach and remove the contents.

2. Pull out the quill.

3. Peel off the slimy covering from the wings inwards.

4. Clean the tentacles by running your fingers repeatedly through them. Little round suckers will fall off that look a bit like plastic.

5. Once the squid is cleaned, cut the tentacles off and cut them into a length that will be easy to eat. Cut the body into strips.

If that sounds too difficult or you are short of time, you can buy frozen pre-cleaned squid but it often has a rubbery or occasionally spongy texture which comes from the process used commercially to strip the slimy skin off. Fresh is always best so do give it a try.

🦁 Honey Tamarind Roast Duck

Serves 4

Duck is one meat that will only respond well to a specific cooking method. If you don't know what you're doing it can end up tough and dry. This method will not only ensure that your duck doesn't dry out, it will also get rid of a lot of the fat that can make duck greasy.

SPICE RUB
1 teaspoon fennel seeds, toasted and finely ground
1 teaspoon ground aniseed
1 teaspoon allspice berries, finely ground
1 teaspoon black peppercorns, finely ground
2 teaspoons mixed peppercorns, finely ground
1½ teaspoons salt

TAMARIND PASTE
4 tablespoons tamarind concentrate
2 cloves garlic, peeled and roughly chopped
2 spring onions, roughly chopped
¾-inch piece ginger root, peeled and roughly chopped
2 tablespoons honey
juice of 1 lime

DUCK
1 x 4 lb duck
3 spring onions, washed
12 cups chicken or duck stock

fresh asparagus spears, woody ends removed, blanched, to serve
steamed white rice to serve
Vietnamese mint to garnish

1. To prepare the spice rub, combine all the ingredients, mix well and set aside.

2. To make the tamarind paste, soak the tamarind concentrate in 6 tablespoons of hot water until softened. Strain to achieve 4 tablespoons tamarind water.

3. Place the tamarind water in a food processor along with the garlic, spring onion, ginger, honey, and lime juice and process to a paste.

4. Wash and pat dry the duck. Trim any excess fat from the duck and prick the skin with a fork.

5. Spoon 2 teaspoons of the spice rub into the cavity of the duck, add half the tamarind paste and the spring onions, and sew up the duck using either a needle and thread or wooden skewers. (The needle and thread leave less obvious marks once cooked.)

6. Place the duck in a large stockpot with the stock over gentle heat and simmer, uncovered, for 45 minutes. Remove the duck from the pan, reserving the stock. Pat dry and set aside to cool. When the duck is cool enough to handle, use your fingers to rub the skin all over in order to eliminate any fat bubbles under the skin. The fat will come out through the pores of the skin so let it run off or use a paper towel to remove as much excess as possible. Rub the remaining spice mixture over the surface and set aside. (All this can be done a day in advance if preferred.) Refrigerate both the duck and stock.

7. When preparing to serve, preheat the oven to 450°F/230°C (or as hot as your oven will reach).

8. Skim the fat from the stock, retaining 1 tablespoon. Discard the rest or freeze for future use. Place the reserved fat in a roasting tray and melt in the oven for 3–4 minutes. Carefully remove the hot tray from the oven and spread out the melted fat so it is evenly distributed. Place the duck, breast side up, in the tray and roast for 20 minutes until golden brown, basting twice during this time. Remove from the oven and brush the surface of the duck with the remaining tamarind paste. Return to the oven and cook for a further 4 minutes, keeping a watchful eye on it to avoid burning.

9. Remove the duck from the oven and rest it for 10–15 minutes prior to carving.

10. Serve with fresh blanched asparagus and steamed white rice. Garnish with Vietnamese mint.

Moorish Swimming Rabbit

Serves 4

This recipe is perfect on a cold winter's night. It's deliciously complemented with an almond milk sauce, which requires a fair bit of whisking but is well worth the effort.

RABBIT
4 tablespoons grapeseed oil
1 rabbit, well cleaned and jointed
1 cup Spanish red wine, such as a Tempranillo, or an Italian Chianti
1 cup water
2 large red onions, peeled and finely chopped
2 bay leaves
3 cloves
1 teaspoon salt
½ teaspoon freshly ground black pepper

SAUCE
⅓ cup ground almonds
3 egg yolks, beaten
1¼ cups whole milk
½ cup brown sugar

4 thick slices sourdough bread to serve
2 tablespoons olive oil to serve
ground cinnamon to garnish

1. To prepare the rabbit, heat the oil in a heavy-based saucepan and brown the rabbit joints. Add the remaining ingredients and bring to a boil. Reduce the heat, cover and simmer for 1 hour. Remove the lid for the last 10–15 minutes to allow the sauce to reduce. Lift out the cooked rabbit, set aside in a warm place, and pour the cooking juices into a bowl.

2. To prepare the sauce, combine the ground almonds, egg yolks, milk, and sugar in a bowl and whisk together until pale and frothy.

3. Bring a saucepan half-filled with water to a boil. Position the bowl containing the almond mixture over the pan and add the rabbit juices. Whisk until thick.

4. Fry the bread slices in the olive oil until golden brown. Transfer to 4 serving plates.

5. Top the fried bread with rabbit pieces and spoon over some of the sauce leaving the remainder to serve at the table. Dust each plate with a little cinnamon and serve.

Overleaf (left): Honey Tamarind Roast Duck; (right) Syrian Poached Chicken on Barley (recipe page 80)

🦁 Syrian Poached Chicken on Barley

Serves 4

Very little preparation is required for this dish and the long cooking time means you can have it bubbling away while you are doing other things. Not only delicious, this dish is also extremely good for you.

CHICKEN STOCK
1 x 3 lb free-range or organic chicken, well washed
2 red onions, peeled and halved
1 bulb garlic, left whole but with the top chopped off to let the flavors out
2 cinnamon sticks
10 allspice berries
2 teaspoons cumin seeds
1 teaspoon salt
5 black peppercorns
½ bunch Italian (flat-leaf) parsley
2 sticks celery, roughly chopped

BARLEY
2 tablespoons butter
1 cup barley, washed and drained well
1 small white onion, peeled and finely chopped
1 stick celery, finely diced
6 cloves garlic, reserved from the stock, peeled and crushed
2½ cups chicken stock
2 cups lightly cooked fresh fava beans (or defrosted from frozen), shelled
juice of 1 lemon
ground sumac to garnish
plain unsweetened yogurt

1. To prepare the chicken stock, combine all the ingredients in a large stockpot and cover with water. Bring to a boil, cover, reduce the heat and simmer for 1 hour. Using a slotted spoon, lift out the garlic bulb and when cool enough to handle, separate and reserve six cloves. Lift out the chicken and set aside with the stock to cool.

2. To prepare the barley, heat the butter in a heavy-based saucepan and add the barley, toasting it as the heat increases and the butter melts. Add the onion, celery, and garlic and mix well. Cook for 2 minutes or until the onion softens. Ladle in the stock and stir. Reduce the heat to a simmer and cook for 25–30 minutes, uncovered, stirring occasionally, until the barley is soft. (This can be done ahead of time and then reheated when required.)

3. Taste to check seasoning and adjust accordingly.

4. While the barley is cooking, remove the cooked chicken from the bones in largish pieces.

5. Once the barley is ready, stir in the fava beans and squeeze over the lemon juice.

6. Serve the barley onto plates. Top with chunks of cooked chicken and a sprinkling of sumac and serve immediately with yogurt on the side.

Andalusian Roasted Lamb

Serves 4

This Moorish-inspired dish is delicate in flavor but does need regular basting while cooking to keep the meat moist.

10 pitted prunes
1 tablespoon raisins or currants
8 dried figs
4 cups water
2 cups rich but not tannic red wine such as a Spanish Rioja
1 teaspoon sugar
10 allspice berries
2 cinnamon sticks
1 teaspoon ground cinnamon
2 bay leaves
6 black peppercorns
½ nutmeg, freshly ground
3 cloves garlic, peeled and roughly chopped
¾-inch piece ginger root, peeled and finely chopped
1 x 1 lb 8 oz boned leg of lamb
sea salt and freshly ground black pepper
extra virgin olive oil

1. Combine the dried fruit, water, wine, sugar, spices, garlic, and ginger in a large saucepan and mix well. Cook over low heat for 30 minutes or until the fruit has softened. Set aside to cool.

2. Preheat the oven to 450°F/230°C.

3. Drain the cooled fruit, reserving the liquid. Place the fruit mix onto the meat. Roll up the lamb, squashing in the fruit at the sides and tie with string. Place in a shallow roasting pan and sprinkle with the salt, pepper, and a little olive oil. Roast for 2–3 minutes to brown and seal the meat.

4. Pour a large ladleful of the reserved fruit cooking liquid over the meat. Reduce the oven temperature to 375°F/190°C and roast the meat for 45–60 minutes, depending on how well cooked you like it, basting every 10–15 minutes with the remaining fruit liquid to moisten and flavor the meat.

5. Remove the lamb from the oven and allow to stand for at least 10 minutes before carving. Then slice finely and stack the fruits on top.

6. Serve as part of a larger menu or with a salad of crisp summer leaves and herbs. You can use any remaining juices in the pan as a flavor base for couscous to serve with the lamb.

🦁 Saffron Wedding Rice

Serves 6

A cross between a rice pudding and a baked savory rice dish, this recipe, known in Iran as *tahcheen*, has comfort food written all over it. It would be a shame to serve it with anything that might detract from its lovely color so consider serving it with pumpkin.

½ teaspoon white sugar
½ teaspoon saffron threads
6 oz plain Greek-style yogurt
2 eggs
1 white onion, peeled and grated
12 cardamom pods, crushed to remove seeds, then seeds toasted and finely ground
3 teaspoons caraway seeds, toasted and finely ground
1 nutmeg, freshly grated
2 mace blades, toasted gently then finely ground
1 teaspoon fennel seeds, toasted and finely ground
8 boneless chicken thighs, skin removed, cut into bite-sized pieces
½ cup olive oil
2⅖ cups white short-grain rice, soaked in cold water for 1 hour, then drained
8 tablespoons butter, cubed
extra saffron threads to garnish

1. Grind the sugar and saffron threads together using a mortar and pestle. Transfer to a small bowl and add 4 tablespoons of warm water. Set aside until required.

2. In another bowl mix together the yogurt and eggs and stir in the onion and the remaining ground spices. Season to taste. Add the saffron and water mix, followed by the chicken. Mix well and set aside to marinate for 2 hours in the refrigerator.

3. Preheat the oven to 325°F/160°C.

4. Grease a large oven safe casserole dish that has a lid with olive oil, then layer one-third of the drained rice in the bottom of the dish and top with half the yogurt mix followed by half the chicken. Repeat, finishing with a layer of rice. Using a teaspoon, push down on the rice to create some deep indentations and fill each with a cube of butter. Cover with a clean tea towel and place the lid on top.

5. Bake for 50 minutes.

6. If possible, turn out the contents of the dish on a serving platter and serve upside down. Alternatively, spoon out the mix so that the crispy rice is on top and garnish with saffron threads.

𝒜 Fennel-coated Snapper with Lemon Parsley Sauce

Serves 4

A salt coating is a great way to cook fish as it keeps the moisture trapped inside. Don't use expensive artisan-style sea salt for the crust, rather, buy the coarse variety in bulk. Serve with a watercress salad or with crusty bread and a selection of chutneys.

SNAPPER
6 lb 9 oz coarse sea salt
2 egg whites, lightly beaten
6 tablespoons fennel seeds
6 lb 9 oz snapper, gutted and descaled

SAUCE
finely grated zest and juice of 1 lemon
6 tablespoons finely chopped Italian (flat-leaf) parsley
½ cup pine nuts, toasted and roughly chopped
4 hard-boiled eggs, peeled and coarsely chopped
½ cup extra virgin olive oil
3 tablespoons cider vinegar
½ teaspoon sea salt
½ teaspoon freshly ground black pepper

1. Preheat the oven to 465°F/240°C.
2. Mix together the salt and egg whites until well combined.
3. Place a layer of egg white and salt mix in the bottom of a roasting dish large enough to hold the fish. Sprinkle half the fennel seeds over the layer of salt, then place the fish on top. Sprinkle the remaining fennel seeds over the fish and cover the fish with the remaining egg white and salt mix. Pack the remaining salt over and around the fish.
4. Bake for 1 hour or until the salt has formed a hard crust around the fish.
5. While the fish is cooking, make the sauce. Place the lemon juice, parsley, pine nuts, and eggs in a bowl and mix to combine, adding the olive oil and vinegar a little at a time. Mix in the lemon zest, salt, and pepper. Taste and add more salt if required.
6. Transfer to a serving jug or bowl and refrigerate until ready to serve.
7. Serve the fish at the table in the tray it was cooked in. Chip away at the top layer of the salt crust to reveal the fish for diners to help themselves. Place the sauce on the side in a jug and serve with a fresh watercress salad or as part of a summer mezze.

🦁 Spicy Chocolate Ginger Tart

This is the recipe to use when you have to bake a cake, but time constraints don't allow you to risk an unknown recipe. Sometimes I cook it for longer so it is firmer and crispy, and other times I bake it a little less when I want a softer, fudgy result.

1½ cups good quality dark chocolate, finely chopped
6 tablespoons butter, cut into small pieces
¾ cup superfine sugar
3 free-range eggs at room temperature
7 cloves, toasted and finely ground
1 teaspoon whole fennel seeds, toasted and finely ground
2 teaspoons whole caraway seed, toasted and finely ground
¾-inch piece ginger root, peeled and finely grated
1¼ cups all-purpose flour
¼ teaspoon salt
4 teaspoons baking powder
1 cup roasted blanched almonds, crushed
finely grated zest of 1 lemon
½ cup milk

1. Preheat the oven to 350°F/180°C.

2. Combine the chocolate and butter in a bowl and position it over a saucepan quarter-filled with water over a medium heat. Make sure the water doesn't touch the bottom of the bowl. Heat until the chocolate has melted and there are no lumps. Stir occasionally to avoid overheating (which is easy to do if you don't keep an eye on things). Set aside to cool.

3. Beat together the sugar, eggs, and spices in a large bowl until thick. Add the chocolate butter mix and beat for 2 minutes. Sift in the flour, salt, and baking powder. Fold in the nuts, lemon zest, and milk.

4. Pour into a well-greased 9½-inch tart pan with a removable base and bake for 25–30 minutes for a softer, fudge-like tart or 45 minutes for a firmer, crisper result.

5. Allow to cool completely before removing from the tart pan.

6. Cut into thin slices or thick wedges, as desired, and serve with whipped cream.

🏵 Sweet Bunelos with Zesty Lime Curd

Makes about 20–25 bunelos

These choux pastry treats take a bit of effort, but the results are well worth it. They are perfect for afternoon tea, so get out the good china and invest in some high-grade tea to really enjoy them.

ZESTY LIME CURD
5 egg yolks, lightly beaten
½ cup superfine sugar
¼ cup freshly squeezed lime juice
⅛ cup freshly squeezed orange juice
finely grated zest of 1 lime
8 tablespoons unsalted butter, cubed

BUNELOS
2 teaspoons cinnamon
½ nutmeg, freshly grated
seeds from ½ vanilla bean (reserve pod for another use)
½ cup all-purpose flour, sifted
⅓ cup water
4 tablespoons extra virgin olive oil
1 teaspoon superfine sugar
pinch salt
½ teaspoon finely grated lemon zest
2 large eggs at room temperature, lightly beaten
whipped cream to serve

1. To make curd, beat the egg yolks and sugar together until pale. Stir in all the juice and zest.

2. Position the bowl over a saucepan half-filled with water. Make sure the bottom of the bowl does not touch the water. Bring the water to a simmer, stirring the mixture from time to time to help dissolve the sugar and gently cook the egg.

3. Whisk in the butter, one cube at a time. Gently cook for 8 minutes without boiling to prevent the curd splitting, until the mixture coats the back of a spoon and when you draw the spoon through it leaves a trail. It can sometimes take a little longer depending on factors such as egg size and moisture in the sugar, but keep stirring gently and do not allow it to boil. Keep doing the spoon test – it should be quite clear once the mixture has cooked and thickened sufficiently.

4. When the mixture is cooked, plunge the bowl into a sinkful of cold water to stop the cooking process. Set aside to cool, then pack into a jar or bowl ready for use. (If made ahead of time, store in the refrigerator until you are ready to use.)

5. When you are ready to make the bunelos, preheat the oven to 425°F/220°C.

6. Mix together the spices, including the vanilla seeds, and flour and set aside.

7. Combine the water, oil, sugar, salt, and zest in a saucepan and place over medium heat, stirring to dissolve the sugar. Bring to boiling point, then remove from the heat. Stir in the flour and spice mix and keep stirring until a smooth paste is formed. Return to a gentle heat and cook for another 5 minutes, stirring continuously – the oil will separate out if it gets too hot. Once a film begins to form on the base of the saucepan, remove from the heat and mix in the eggs, one at a time, using a wooden spoon. Beat the mixture for a few minutes or until it forms a glossy, thick, smooth batter.

8. Line two oven trays with baking paper. Spoon teaspoonful-sized blobs of the mix onto the paper, ensuring there is at least 1½ inches between each to allow them to spread.

9. Bake a maximum of 2 trays at a time for 10 minutes until they begin to puff up, then reduce the heat to 350°F/180°C and cook for a further 20 minutes until crisp and golden.

10. Remove from the oven and pierce each bunelo to enable steam to escape. Transfer to a cake rack to cool.

11. Repeat this process with remaining batter, ensuring the temperature of the oven is back up to 425°F/220°C before baking.

12. To serve, gently split the bunelos in half and fill one half with the curd and some whipped cream. Top with the other half and serve immediately.

NOTE: You can make a savory version by replacing the spices with ground cumin and paprika and filling the bunelos with a slice of delicate soft goat's cheese and a dollop of herb-heavy aïoli.

✿ *Sunday Morning Apple Pikelets*

Makes about 15

The smell of apples cooking in butter is a beautiful thing. Try these pikelets for a change when you fancy pancakes. If buttermilk is not available, add 1 tablespoon of lemon juice to every cup of milk required.

STEWED APPLE
²⁄₅ cup muscovado sugar
6 whole cloves
seeds from 1 vanilla bean (reserve pod for another use)
2 apples, peeled and finely sliced
2 teaspoons ground cinnamon
2 tablespoons water

PIKELETS
3 eggs, beaten
1¼ cups buttermilk
3³⁄₅ cups all-purpose flour
1 heaped teaspoon baking soda
1 heaped teaspoon cream of tartar
½ teaspoon salt
butter for frying

1. A day ahead, mix the sugar with the cloves and the vanilla seeds and set aside to infuse. The next day, remove the cloves.

2. Mix half the infused sugar in a saucepan with the apple slices and add the cinnamon and water. Cook over a medium heat for 20 minutes or until softened. Allow to cool. Drain off any excess liquid, then break up the apple slices using a masher.

3. To make the pikelets, add the eggs one at a time to the buttermilk and stir well. Sift in the dry ingredients, mixing thoroughly. Add the stewed apple mixture to the batter and mix well.

4. Heat a heavy-based frying pan and grease with a little butter. Add spoonfuls of the batter to form pikelets 2½ inches in diameter. Turn over when bubbles appear on the uncooked surface and cook for another 2 minutes. (The apple adds extra moisture so take care to cook for long enough to avoid little pockets of uncooked batter around the apple.)

5. Cook in batches and keep warm in the oven until ready to serve along with substantial slabs of cold butter. Serve hot.

Arab Orange Blossom and Sumac Pancakes

Makes 10–15

The plain version of these pancakes, known as *ataif*, harks back to medieval times for the purpose of breaking the Ramadan fast. For a variation, omit the syrup and serve with stewed fruit and some thick Greek-style yogurt – perfect for a lazy weekend breakfast.

PANCAKES
5 teaspoons active dry yeast
3 cups warm water
2 teaspoons sugar
2⅔ cups all-purpose flour, sifted
4 teaspoons ground sumac
seeds from 18 cardamom pods, toasted and finely ground

SYRUP
1¼ cups water
2¼ cups superfine sugar
juice of 1 lemon
2 tablespoons orange blossom water

grapeseed oil for cooking
3 handfuls shelled and toasted pistachio nuts and Greek-style yogurt to serve

1. To make the pancakes, combine the yeast with approximately ¾ cup of the warm water. Stir in the sugar and leave the mixture to froth for 5 minutes.

2. Sprinkle in the flour, then add the rest of the water, the sumac, and freshly ground cardamom. Mix, using a whisk, until a thick batter is formed.

3. Cover with plastic wrap and set aside to rest in a warm place for 1 hour, after which the batter should be elastic, bubbly, and very sticky to the touch.

4. To make the syrup, heat the water in a saucepan and stir in the sugar. Bring to a boil, then reduce the heat and stir in the lemon juice. Cook for a further 10–15 minutes until the sugar syrup thickens enough to coat the back of a spoon. Add the orange blossom water and stir well. Remove from the heat and cool.

5. Heat a little of the oil in a heavy-based frying pan.

6. Using a ladle, spoon out sufficient batter to create several pancakes each 1–2 inches in diameter. Cook the pancakes until they bubble at the sides, then flip them to cook the underside for the same amount of time. You want them golden-brown but not burnt. However, take care not to undercook them as they will be too heavy.

7. Keep cooked pancakes warm in a low oven at 300°F/150°C while the rest cook.

8. Dip each pancake in the syrup, spoon over some yogurt, and sprinkle with pistachio nuts and serve immediately.

NOTE: The syrup can be made days in advance and chilled until needed.

Spiced Nights

Fragrant, heady, and evocative of desert nights under the stars,
the dishes in this chapter are rich with the scent of cinnamon
and meat slow-cooked in the tagine, poached fruits laced with
rose water, and much more besides.

🦁 Hot Mezze Hummus

Serves 4 as part of a feast

A specialty from the mountainous area in the east of Turkey, this rich and garlic-heavy baked hummus begs to be eaten with large hunks of flatbread.

2 cups dried chickpeas, soaked in several changes of water, rinsed
²/₃ cup olive oil
finely grated zest and juice of 2 lemons
3 tablespoons tahini
15 oz thick Greek-style yogurt
8 cloves garlic, roasted in their skins until soft, cooled and peeled
3 teaspoons toasted and finely ground cumin seeds
3 teaspoons coriander seeds, toasted and finely ground
1 teaspoon ground turmeric
2 teaspoons salt
1 teaspoon freshly ground black pepper
3 tablespoons chopped almonds
2 teaspoons sesame seeds
4 tablespoons butter
2 tablespoons ground sumac
juice of 1 lemon to serve

1. Cook the chickpeas in plenty of water in a large saucepan for 40–60 minutes or until softened. Remove from the heat, rinse well then remove and discard the skins.

2. Preheat the oven to 400°F/200°C.

3. Transfer the drained, skinned chickpeas to a food processor and process (in batches if necessary) with the olive oil, lemon zest and juice, tahini, and yogurt. Add the garlic, spices, salt, and pepper and process until well mixed and smooth.

4. Spoon the hummus into a shallow oven safe dish.

5. Quickly toast the almonds and sesame seeds in a dry pan until just brown, then add the butter. Once the butter has melted, add the sumac.

6. Pour the nut and sumac mixture over the hummus evenly.

7. Bake for 25 minutes or until most of the butter has been absorbed.

8. Squeeze over the lemon juice. Serve with plenty of flatbread for scooping up the creamy hummus.

Eggplant Rolls with Honey, Mint, and Sesame Seeds

Serves 3–4 as an appetizer

Tastes of fresh mint and honey are complemented by the soft texture of the eggplant. Serve as an appetizer or as part of a mezze with other small dishes.

> 2 large eggplants, tops trimmed, cut lengthwise into ¼-inch strips
> vegetable or grapeseed oil for baking
> 1 teaspoon iodized salt
> 6 tablespoons good quality honey
> 6 tablespoons well washed and finely chopped mint
> 6 teaspoons sesame seeds, toasted in a dry pan until brown
> juice of 1 lemon

1. Preheat the oven to 350°F/180°C.
2. Arrange the eggplant strips with a little space between each. Moisten each with a little vegetable oil and sprinkle over the salt.
3. Bake for 15 minutes or until brown and soft. Remove from the oven and cool, patting them with some paper towels to remove excess oil.
4. Drizzle the eggplant strips with the honey, then sprinkle with some of the mint and some of the sesame seeds. Roll up each slice and place on a serving plate. Squeeze over the lemon juice and scatter the remaining mint and sesame seeds over the top.
5. Serve immediately.

❧ Spice Merchant Soup

Makes enough for 10 journeys

Amazingly fragrant and restorative, this soup will take you on a taste journey that can be almost as good as the real thing.

SPICE BAG
1 tablespoon toasted fenugreek seeds
3 teaspoons toasted cumin seeds
2 cinnamon sticks
1 teaspoon allspice berries, cracked
3 teaspoons toasted coriander seeds
1 teaspoon toasted fennel seeds
1 teaspoon nigella seeds

STOCK
¼ cup olive oil
3 red onions, peeled and coarsely chopped
3 sticks celery, coarsely chopped
3 carrots, peeled and coarsely chopped
2 leeks, well washed, trimmed and coarsely chopped
1 garlic bulb, whole
2 lb pumpkin, peeled, seeded, and cut into chunks
6 parsnips, peeled and coarsely chopped
3 potatoes, peeled and coarsely chopped
2 teaspoons ground turmeric
8 cups water
2 x 2 lb free-range or organic chickens
fresh cilantro leaves to garnish

1. To make the spice bag, place all the ingredients on a piece of muslin and tie up the corners to form a bag.

2. To make the stock, heat the olive oil in a large heavy-based stockpot. Add the vegetables and cook for 3–4 minutes or until lightly browned. Add the turmeric, mixing in well. Add the water and chickens and bring to a boil. Reduce the heat and simmer, covered, for 1 hour.

3. Add the spice bag to the stockpot at the end of the first hour of cooking time, stirring well to release the flavors. Cook over a low simmering heat for a further hour.

4. At the end of the cooking time, lift out the chickens and set aside to cool. Remove the flesh when it is cool enough to handle.

5. Using a slotted spoon, remove the spice bag and garlic bulb from the pot. Using a potato masher, coarsely crush the vegetables until chunky. Return the chicken meat to the pot and bring back to a simmer.

6. Taste to check seasonings and adjust as required.

7. Serve in bowls garnished with the cilantro alongside toasted flatbread.

Egyptian Chickpea and Pumpkin Fritters

Serves 8 as part of a mezze

Chickpeas are the staple food of Egypt and are often used in Italy and Spain for stews and soups. Requiring at least 8 hours of soaking time and a fairly long cooking time they should be soft enough to squash between your fingers before being added to any dish.

1 cup chickpeas, soaked in several changes of cold water, rinsed
1 lb 2 oz pumpkin, peeled and chopped into chunks for roasting
8 cloves garlic
grapeseed oil for roasting
2 teaspoons ground turmeric
3 teaspoons cumin seeds, toasted and finely ground
3 teaspoons coriander seeds, toasted and finely ground
3 teaspoons garam masala spice blend
1 teaspoon ground chili flakes
2 teaspoons ajowan, toasted and finely ground
1½ cups all-purpose flour
5 teaspoons baking powder
2 teaspoons salt
3 tablespoons plain yogurt
2 lemons, cut into wedges

1. Cook the chickpeas in plenty of water in a large saucepan for 40–60 minutes or until softened. Remove from the heat, rinse well then remove and discard the skins.

2. Preheat the oven to 350°F/180°C.

3. Place the pumpkin and unpeeled garlic in a roasting dish with a little oil and roast for 20 minutes until soft. Remove from the oven and set aside to cool. Leave the oven on.

4. Grease an oven tray and set aside.

5. Place the cooked chickpeas in a food processor and pulse until roughly chopped. Do this in several batches if necessary so the food processor is not overcrowded.

6. Transfer the chickpea mixture to a large bowl. Add the pumpkin, peeled garlic, and the remaining ingredients.

7. Using your hands, mix everything together, roughly mashing the pumpkin in the process.

8. Form small balls of the mixture and place on the greased tray. Flatten the balls slightly – they should now be about 1½ inches in diameter.

9. Bake for 10–15 minutes until slightly browned and crisp.

10. Serve warm or cold with yogurt and wedges of fresh lemon as part of a mezze, with a simple green salad or stuffed into pita bread.

🦁 Seville Duck with Oranges and Olives

Serves 4

An Andalusian specialty, this dish features Seville oranges. If these are not available, any other variety will do.

4 duck marylands (thigh and leg portion together)
2 tablespoons grapeseed oil
3 cloves garlic, peeled and finely chopped
2 teaspoons whole coriander seeds, toasted and finely ground
1 cinnamon stick
2 sprigs rosemary
2 tablespoons fresh oregano leaves
2 oranges, quartered and seeds removed
1 lemon, peeled, quartered and seeds removed
1 tablespoon honey
15 green olives, preferably Spanish
½ cup manzanilla or dry sherry
1 teaspoon salt
1 teaspoon freshly ground black pepper
½ cup water
orange slices to garnish
steamed white rice

1. Score the skin on the duck in a criss-cross fashion very gently so as not to cut into the flesh. This helps release the fat.

2. Heat a heavy-based casserole dish with the oil and brown the duck. Remove and set aside.

3. Add the garlic, coriander seeds, and cinnamon and stir to infuse and soften. Add the remaining ingredients except the orange slices and bring to a boil. Reduce the heat and return the duck to the pan. Simmer for 35–40 minutes until the sauce has reduced and is of a syrupy consistency. Taste to check seasonings and adjust as required. Lift out the duck and set aside to keep warm.

4. Increase the heat until the sauce has further reduced and is quite thick.

5. Serve the sauce drizzled on top of the duck, garnished with fresh slices of orange and some steamed white rice.

🦁 Stuffed and Tied Lamb

Serves 4–6

Lamb carries flavors well so spices are an ideal match. Ask your butcher for a boned lamb shoulder with the skin on. You may find it difficult to master tying the meat neatly, but the string only needs to hold the meat together – you can cut it off before anyone sees it!

STUFFING
2 tablespoons grapeseed oil
1 white onion, peeled and finely chopped
6 cloves garlic, peeled and finely chopped
3 green cardamom pods, crushed to remove seeds, then seeds toasted and finely ground
1 cinnamon stick split in half lengthwise
3 teaspoons cumin seeds, toasted and finely ground
a pinch of saffron threads, soaked in 3 tablespoons warm water
1 tablespoon honey
2 teaspoons salt
1 teaspoon freshly ground black pepper
1 cup cooked white rice
4 tablespoons orange blossom water
finely grated zest and juice of 1 orange

LAMB
4 lb 6 oz boneless lamb leg, trimmed of any visible fat
3 tablespoons grapeseed oil
2 teaspoons sea salt
2 teaspoons freshly ground black pepper

plain natural yogurt and fresh greens to serve
lemon and mint to garnish

1. Preheat the oven to 350°F/180°C.

2. To make the stuffing, heat the oil in a frying pan and cook the onion and garlic for about 2 minutes until softened. Stir in the spices and cook for a further 2 minutes.

3. Tip into a large bowl. Add all the remaining ingredients and mix well.

4. Place the lamb on the bench, skin side down. Place handfuls of stuffing down the middle of the meat. There may be an excess of stuffing, but try and fit on as much as you can. Fold the sides of the meat to the middle and roll up. Secure with string.

5. Rub grapeseed oil, salt, and pepper over the meat. Place in a well-oiled baking dish in the oven for 45–50 minutes depending on how you like your lamb.

6. Allow to rest before beginning to carve.

7. Arrange any excess stuffing you have on the bottom of a large platter and lay the carved slices of lamb on top. Slice the lamb on the diagonal so each slice shows the saffron-tinted stuffing.

8. Serve immediately with side dishes of yogurt and fresh greens.

Moroccan Chermoula-baked Fish Salad

Serves 4 as part of a mezze or 2-3 on its own

There are many variations of chermoula, but the chili element is a constant. Zesty and tangy, yet musky with spice, it is a great addition to so many dishes.

CHERMOULA
8 teaspoons cumin seeds, toasted and finely ground
3 teaspoons coriander seeds, toasted and finely ground
4 teaspoons sweet paprika
3 teaspoons ground ginger
4 teaspoons ground turmeric
4 cloves garlic, peeled and finely chopped
2 whole habañero chilies, seeded and finely chopped
juice and zest of 3 lemons
½ cup olive oil
1 teaspoon salt
8 tablespoons finely chopped fresh cilantro
4 tablespoons finely chopped fresh mint

1 large fish, e.g. snapper, weighing about 1 lb, gutted and scaled

SALAD
3 young fennel bulbs, trimmed, washed and cut into slivers
3 red onions, peeled and cut into quarters
1 bunch watercress, picked over and woody stems discarded
2–3 tablespoons good-quality extra virgin olive oil
2 tablespoons roughly chopped fresh cilantro to garnish

1. Combine all the ingredients for the chermoula in a bowl. Mix together well and store in the refrigerator until required.

2. To prepare the fish, first preheat the oven to 400°F/200°C.

3. Place the fish in a large oven dish. Fill the cavity with some chermoula and spread the rest over the top.

4. Bake for 15–20 minutes. Remove from the oven and set the fish aside to cool. (If desired, the fish can be served whole at this stage with accompaniments of your choice.)

5. To prepare the salad, reduce the oven temperature to 350°F/180°C. Place the fennel and onion with a little oil in a clean oven dish and carefully toss to coat. Roast the vegetables for 12 minutes. Remove from the oven and set aside to cool with the fish.

6. Either serve the fish whole at the table with salad separately or, when the fish is cool enough to handle, remove the flesh from the bones and mix with the salad. Pour over any liquid from the roasting dish and lubricate further with extra virgin olive oil.

7. Serve on individual plates or a large shared platter and garnish with cilantro leaves.

NOTE: This recipe makes more chermoula than is necessary for this dish. Pack extra into an airtight jar and store in the refrigerator for up to 6 weeks. Serve with breads or add a spoonful to soups and marinades.

🦁 *Fragrant Desert Tagine with Couscous*

Serves 6–8 people as part of a Moroccan dinner

Extremely versatile, couscous is fast and easy to prepare. Made from semolina flour that is formed into a paste, dried and sieved, it's a big part of the Algerian and Tunisian diets, although its true home is Morocco where it is the national dish.

TAGINE

2 tablespoons butter
2 tablespoons whole cumin seeds, toasted and ground
2 tablespoons whole coriander seeds, toasted and ground
1 teaspoon ground sumac
3 teaspoons whole ajowan seeds, toasted and ground
2 cinnamon sticks
2 teaspoons ground turmeric
10 cloves garlic, peeled and finely chopped
4 lamb shanks
4 chicken thighs
5 large ripe tomatoes or 1 x 14 oz can peeled tomatoes
a pinch of saffron threads, soaked in ½ cup warm water for 20 minutes, drained
1 mild fresh red chili
3 liters water
1 small pumpkin, peeled, seeded and cut into 1½-inch cubes
3 red peppers, halved and seeded
2 large red onions, peeled and cut into eighths
1²/₃ cups baby carrots, well washed
1 large eggplant, cut into 1½-inch cubes
²/₃ cup dried chickpeas, soaked in several changes of cold water overnight, rinsed well and cooked in
    cold water for 25–35 minutes (or 1 x 14 oz can chickpeas, well rinsed)
½ cup dried pitted dates
2 preserved lemons, skin removed and cut into strips
2 tablespoons salt
1 tablespoon freshly ground black pepper

COUSCOUS

4 cups couscous
8 tablespoons butter
5 cups tagine broth, heated

fresh cilantro leaves and lemon juice to serve

1. Preheat the oven to 335°F/170°C.

2. Melt the butter over medium heat in a tagine or large heavy-based casserole dish with a lid. Add the cumin, coriander seeds, sumac, ajowan, cinnamon, turmeric, and garlic. Sauté for 2 minutes before adding the lamb and chicken. Stir to coat and cook for 5–6 minutes or until well browned. Add the tomatoes, saffron and its soaking water, chili, and the water.

3. Transfer to the oven and cook, covered, for 30 minutes.

4. Remove from the oven and stir well. Add the pumpkin, red pepper, onions, carrots, and eggplant and cook, covered, for a further 2 hours, reducing the oven to 350°F/150°C.

5. Remove from the oven again, add the chickpeas, dates, and preserved lemon and cook for a further 30 minutes. Stir well and add seasoning. If the tagine is looking a little dry at this point, stir in about 1 cup of water and allow to simmer for another 15–20 minutes. The total cooking time will be about 3 hours over low heat. When cooked, set the tagine aside to cool.

6. When cool, remove the meat from the bones and shred into bite-sized pieces. Return the shredded meat to the tagine.

7. Reheat gently on low heat to a simmer. Remove some of the broth to use when preparing the couscous, then reduce the remaining tagine liquid until it is thick but runny enough to moisten the couscous when served.

8. To prepare the couscous, toast it lightly in a dry saucepan or in the oven in a baking dish until it begins to color (2–3 minutes) to give it a nutty flavor and to help it absorb more fluid later on.

9. Melt the butter in a large saucepan and toss the toasted couscous through to coat. Add the broth and cover to steam for 5–10 minutes before fluffing up with a fork.

10. Taste to check seasonings and adjust as required. Spoon out the couscous onto a large platter and top with the tagine. Garnish with fresh cilantro leaves and finish with some freshly squeezed lemon juice.

Handmade Harissa with Roasted Fish

Serves 4

Used as a bread topping, a flavor for couscous, or simply as an accompaniment to grilled meats and fish, harissa is very popular, from parts of the Mediterranean to Africa. Dried rather than fresh chilies are used to give it a warm flavor.

HARISSA
3 whole dried serrano chilies, seeded and finely chopped
3 teaspoons caraway seeds, toasted
3 teaspoons cumin seeds, toasted
2 teaspoons Spanish smoked sweet paprika
5 cloves garlic, peeled
2 teaspoons salt
5 black peppercorns
1 teaspoon dried pink peppercorns
1 teaspoon whole cloves, toasted
6 tablespoons grapeseed oil

ROASTED FISH
juice of 1 lemon
2 tablespoons grapeseed oil
1 lb 10 oz firm white fish, whole or fileted

fresh blanched asparagus, pita bread, and natural yogurt to serve

1. To make the harissa, use a mortar and pestle to grind together all the ingredients except the oil until well amalgamated but still coarse. Add the oil a little at a time to achieve a smooth paste. Pack into a jar ready for use. Store in the refrigerator to marinate for up to 6 months.

2. To prepare the fish, add the lemon juice and extra oil to 3 tablespoons of harissa. Coat the fish well, cover and place in the refrigerator to marinate for up to 2 hours.

3. Grill the fish in a very hot oven until cooked through. This will only take a matter of minutes which will vary depending on the thickness of the fish.

4. Serve immediately with fresh blanched asparagus, pita bread, and a little yogurt to tone down the chili factor.

🦁 Cardamom Cassia and Orange Syrup-baked Cheesecake

Serves 6

Make this decadent treat when oranges are in season. Any extra syrup can be stored for three months in an airtight container in the refrigerator and is great on toast, over vanilla ice cream or, for a savory option, try it with chicken.

SYRUP
2 lb oranges
6 cups white sugar
3 pieces cassia bark, each 2½ inches long
seeds from 30 cardamom pods, softly crushed with a mortar and pestle
5 cups water

BASE
1 package plain biscuits
10 tablespoons butter, melted
finely grated zest of 1 lemon

TOPPING
7 oz cream cheese, softened
3½ oz ricotta cheese
3½ oz mascarpone
4 eggs, separated
²/₃ cup superfine sugar
1 tablespoon all-purpose flour

1. To make the syrup, cut the oranges in half and squeeze out the juice into a large saucepan, reserving the skins. Add the sugar, cassia, cardamom, and water and stir until the sugar has dissolved. Add the orange skins to the pan and bring to a boil. Reduce the heat and simmer for 1 hour. Remove from heat and set aside to cool. When cooled, strain the syrup and discard the orange skins or finely chop some of the orange skins to serve alongside the cheesecake.

2. To make the base, crush the biscuits so that they resemble breadcrumbs. Add the melted butter and lemon zest to the crumbs and mix well. Press into a well-greased 8-inch springform cake pan and chill for at least 2 hours.

3. Preheat oven to 350°F/180°C.

4. To make the topping, combine the cheeses, mixing them with a fork to incorporate. Add the egg yolks and mix again.

5. In a separate bowl, whisk the egg whites until stiff, gradually adding the sugar a spoonful at a time, then add the flour.

6. Add the egg white mixture to the cheese mixture and gently fold to combine. Pour onto the base.

7. Bake in the middle of the oven for 1 hour or until firm to the touch. This may take a little longer in some ovens and you may need to cover the cheesecake with aluminum foil for the last 10 minutes of cooking time to stop it burning. Remove from the oven and cool for 10 minutes before turning out of the pan. Pour over the syrup and serve with extra syrup on hand for those who want it.

NOTE: You can use only cream cheese for the topping if you prefer, or perhaps cream cheese and either ricotta or mascarpone – ricotta adds extra texture while the mascarpone adds a luxurious softness.

🦁 Betrothal Rice Pudding

Serves 4

Once a marriage has been agreed upon by Afghan families, the cooking begins. Sweets are prepared and presented to each family followed by various savory dishes.

 1½ cups short-grain rice, well washed and drained
 6 tablespoons milk
 7 teaspoons superfine sugar
 seeds from 4 cardamom pods, toasted and finely ground
 2 tablespoons raisins
 12 saffron threads, soaked in 5 tablespoons warm water
 1 tablespoon rose water
 1 tablespoon toasted and lightly ground pistachio nuts, plus 1 tablespoon to garnish
 1 tablespoon toasted and lightly ground almonds

1. Place the rice in a large saucepan with enough cold water to cover by 1¼ inches. Bring to a boil over high heat, then simmer for 10 minutes, covered. Remove the lid and stir in the milk, sugar, ground cardamom, raisins, and saffron in the soaking water and return to a boil. Reduce the heat again and cook, covered, for a further 20 minutes then stir in the rose water and ground nuts.

2. Serve in individual dishes, garnished with the extra ground pistachio nuts.

🦁 Arabian White Coffee Ice Cream

Serves 4-6

Coffee and cardamom go well together. Many Arab countries brew coffee this way by adding cardamom to the coffee pot to steep.

 ½ cup freshly roasted coffee beans
 4 cups half & half
 1 cinnamon stick
 seeds from 10 cardamom pods
 2 strips lemon zest about 1½ inches long (use a potato peeler to get thick strips of the right length)
 1 whole nutmeg
 5 egg yolks
 ½ cup light muscovado sugar
 ¼ teaspoon salt

1. Place the coffee beans, half & half, cinnamon, cardamom seeds, lemon zest, and nutmeg in a large saucepan and set aside to infuse for 20 minutes.

2. Place over low heat, stirring occasionally, and gently bring the half & half to just under boiling point. Strain, discarding the spices and zest.

3. Beat the egg yolks with the sugar and salt in a bowl until creamy and pale.

4. Pour the hot cream infusion into the yolk mixture, stirring until it is well incorporated. Return to the pan and heat, stirring constantly, until the mixture coats the back of a spoon and leaves a trail when you run your finger through it.

5. Strain the mixture into a metal bowl and place in the freezer. After 2 hours remove and stir to break up the ice crystals. Repeat this process several times to aerate the ice cream and make it creamy.

6. Remove from the freezer 10 minutes prior to serving to soften.

Saffron Pistachio Parfait

Serves 4

Visually stunning but very easy to make, this winning dessert is perfect to serve after a fragrant, spicy meal.

$^2/_3$ cup whole milk
a pinch of saffron, toasted and crumbled gently using fingertips
4 egg yolks
½ cup superfine sugar
1 cup half & half
$^2/_3$ cup pistachio nuts, toasted

1. Heat the milk and saffron together in a small saucepan and bring almost to a boil. Remove from the heat and set aside for 5–10 minutes to cool and infuse.

2. Beat the egg yolks and sugar together in a bowl using an electric handbeater until the mixture is pale and glossy. Gradually add in the milk and saffron mixture, then return the contents of the bowl to the pan.

3. Gently heat, taking care not to let it boil, stirring occasionally, until the mixture coats the back of a spoon and you can run your finger through it making a pathway.

4. Pour the mixture into a bowl and set aside to cool to room temperature.

5. Whip the half & half to soft peaks. Carefully fold in the cooled saffron milk mixture and the pistachio nuts.

6. Pour into a non-metallic container and freeze for 6–8 hours or overnight.

7. Remove from the freezer 15 minutes before required. Serve with almond wafers.

Winter Blues

The depths of winter can get you down and good nurturing food can bring a great deal of comfort during the bleakest of weather. These recipes serve as a reminder that winter doesn't have to mean sacrificing taste to keep warm. Far from it – winter vegetables are full of flavor and nutrients to see you through those cold-weather blues and, mixed with exotic spices, these dishes are bound to perk you up as well as warm you up.

✖ Winter Blues Thai Soup

Serves 2-3 thoroughly sun-starved people

The flavors of Thai food are a treat in the middle of winter when you would rather be somewhere that's a lot warmer and sunnier.

2 tablespoons vegetable oil
12 shallots, peeled and roughly chopped
4 cups chicken stock
4 sticks lemongrass, tops trimmed and root ends crushed
2-inch piece galangal, peeled and finely sliced
8 small Thai eggplants, trimmed and quartered or use 1 regular purple eggplant, cut into chunks
10 oz pumpkin, peeled, seeded, and cut into chunks
3 cloves garlic, peeled and finely sliced
1 Thai green chili, seeded and finely chopped
1 Thai red chili, seeded and finely chopped
juice of 2 limes
4 kaffir lime leaves, preferably fresh
2 tablespoons fish sauce
1 free-range chicken breast, thinly sliced
1 x 14 oz can coconut milk
1 tablespoon salt
6 tablespoons finely chopped fresh cilantro leaves

9 oz fresh rice stick noodles softened in hot water for 4–5 minutes (or dried rice noodles cooked to package instructions)

1. Heat the oil in a frying pan and fry the shallots for 2–3 minutes until soft and a little brown. Set aside.

2. Pour the chicken stock into a large saucepan and heat. When it has reached simmering point, add the lemongrass, galangal, eggplant, pumpkin, garlic, and green chili. Simmer for 30 minutes.

3. Add the red chili, lime juice, kaffir lime leaves, and fish sauce and allow to infuse for 5 minutes while simmering. Lift out the lemongrass and discard.

4. Add the chicken and coconut milk to the pan and simmer for 2–3 minutes. At this point the pumpkin should have softened to the extent that it falls apart and colors the soup. Taste to check seasonings and adjust as required; you may need a little more lime juice, fish sauce, or salt.

5. Divide the softened noodles between two or three large bowls as required. Spoon in the soup, dividing the chicken and cooked vegetables evenly between the bowls and garnish with the cilantro.

🦁 Cold-winter's-day Parsnip Soup

Serves 4

The lovely woody flavors combined with the cream make for a wintery treat.

  2 lb parsnips, peeled and cut into quarters
  2 white onions, peeled and quartered
  2¼ cups chicken or vegetable stock
  2 teaspoons coriander seeds, toasted and finely ground
  2 teaspoons cumin seeds, toasted and finely ground
  ¼ freshly grated nutmeg
  1 cup half & half
  salt and pepper to taste

1. Place the parsnips and onions in a saucepan and add the stock. Cover and cook until very soft. Add the coriander and cumin and grate in half the nutmeg.

2. Using either a food processor or stick blender, process the vegetables in the stock until smooth.

3. Return the soup to the pan and cook over high heat for 20 minutes to thicken and reduce.

4. Add the half & half and the seasonings. Taste and adjust the seasoning as required. Gently reheat.

5. Serve in bowls with the remaining nutmeg sprinkled on top, accompanied by slices of hot, buttered home-made bread.

🦁 Smoky Beet and Brown Cardamom Soup

Serves 4

Enjoy this gorgeously colored soup with thick toasted slabs of pumpernickel or rye bread and perhaps a few slices of serrano ham on the side.

  3 tablespoons grapeseed oil
  seeds from 1 brown cardamom pod, ground
  seeds from 2 green cardamom pods, toasted and finely ground
  ¾-inch piece fresh turmeric, peeled and finely grated or 1 teaspoon ground turmeric
  2 teaspoons cumin seeds, toasted and finely ground
  2 red onions, peeled and roughly chopped
  3 cloves garlic, peeled and roughly chopped
  1 large Yukon Gold or similar floury potato, peeled, and chopped
  1 lb 10 oz beets, well washed, peeled, and chopped
  4 cups good-quality rich vegetable or chicken stock
  Greek-style yogurt or extra virgin olive oil to garnish

1. In a large saucepan, heat the oil and add the spices. Stir to coat and cook for 1–2 minutes. Add the onion and garlic and cook for 2–3 minutes to soften.

2. Add the potatoes and beets, mixing well before adding the stock. Bring to a boil, reduce the heat and simmer, covered, stirring occasionally, for 45 minutes or until the beets are cooked through.

3. Remove the lid and simmer for a further 10 minutes to allow the soup to reduce a little. Transfer the contents of the pan to a food processor or use a stick blender to process until smooth and thick.

4. Serve in bowls with yogurt or extra virgin olive oil drizzled over.

🌿 Southern Black Bean Soup

Serves 6

The distinctive flavor of black beans sets them apart from the rest of the bean family. They are a staple of South American cuisine.

2½ cups dried black beans, soaked overnight in several changes of cold water
2 bunches fresh cilantro
2 tablespoons grapeseed oil
4 red onions, peeled and quartered
6 cloves garlic, peeled
1 tablespoon whole cumin seeds, toasted and finely ground
1 tablespoon whole coriander seeds, toasted and finely ground
4 dried red chilies, Kashmiri if possible, seeded but left whole
8 cups chicken or vegetable stock
6 sticks celery, roughly chopped
2 carrots, peeled and roughly chopped
3 large potatoes, peeled and roughly chopped
1 leek, trimmed, washed, and roughly chopped
2 bay leaves, dried
1 teaspoon Spanish smoked sweet paprika
⅔ cup crème fraîche to serve

1. Rinse the beans thoroughly before adding enough fresh cold water to cover. Cook uncovered for 40 minutes until soft. Drain, rinse well with cold water, drain again and set aside.

2. Remove the cilantro leaves from the stems and set aside. Discard stems.

3. Heat the oil in a frying pan and sauté the onion and garlic for 3 minutes until softened, then add the cumin, coriander, and chilies. Cook for 2 minutes to allow the flavors to infuse. Set aside.

4. Pour the stock into a large stockpot and add the vegetables. Add the garlic, onion, spice mixture, bay leaves, paprika, and half the fresh cilantro and bring to a boil. Reduce the heat and simmer for 1 hour.

5. Remove the bay leaves and chilies from the pan and discard. Add the beans and the remaining fresh cilantro to the pan. Using a stick blender, purée to form a smooth soup. Simmer gently.

6. Serve with a dollop of crème fraîche on top.

NOTE: If you want to add meat to this hearty dish, try a good old-fashioned free-range bacon hock – the smoky flavors work well with the spices and chili. If you choose to try this, use water rather than stock. The hock will provide plenty of flavor.

🦁 Lamb Cutlets, Spiced Vegetables, and Cauliflower Cream

Serves 4

Cauliflower has had some bad press over the years, but roasted with spices or, as in this case, blended with loads of garlic, it oozes comfort for winter months.

LAMB CUTLETS
2 French lamb racks
2 tablespoons grapeseed oil
zest and juice of 1 lemon
½ teaspoon salt
½ teaspoon freshly ground black pepper

SPICED VEGETABLES
10 cloves garlic
24 black kalamata olives
20 caperberries, well rinsed
10 baby spring onions, trimmed if necessary and well washed
10 baby beets, well washed and trimmed of all but the sprouting tops
½ teaspoon sea salt
½ teaspoon freshly ground black pepper
3 tablespoons grapeseed oil

CAULIFLOWER CREAM
2¼ cups cauliflower, broken into small florets
½ cup half & half
2 cups chicken or vegetable stock
1 sprig thyme
1 teaspoon salt
1 teaspoon freshly ground black pepper
2 tablespoons olive oil
¼ cup ground almonds
¼ nutmeg, freshly grated
2 teaspoons toasted and finely ground caraway seeds
2 teaspoons toasted and finely ground cumin seeds

1. Cut the lamb racks into individual cutlets. Mix together the oil, lemon zest and juice with the salt and pepper. Rub into the chops and set aside for 10–15 minutes.

2. To prepare the spiced vegetables, preheat the oven to 375°F/190°C.

3. Place all the ingredients in a roasting dish and stir so that all are coated in oil. Roast for 15 minutes. The beets will be wonderfully crunchy and the olives will caramelize, becoming softer but deliciously salty. Remove from the oven but keep warm by covering with aluminum foil until ready to serve.

4. Meanwhile, heat a griddle plate or a frying pan. Cook the lamb just before the cauliflower is ready and set aside to rest for 3 minutes or so prior to serving.

5. Place the cauliflower in a saucepan and add the half & half, stock, thyme, salt, and pepper. Cover and cook over medium heat for about 8 minutes or until soft, but not squishy. Using a slotted spoon, lift out the cauliflower and set aside. Increase the heat under the stock and half & half mixture and cook to reduce by half and thicken the liquid for 15 minutes.

6. Process the cauliflower in a blender or food processor with the roasted garlic, almonds, nutmeg, and seeds. Return the cauliflower mixture to the thickened cream sauce and mix well to combine over heat. Cook for a further 3–5 minutes until thick and soupy. Remove the sprig of thyme and discard. Take the pan off the heat and stir in the olive oil. Taste to check seasonings and adjust as required.

7. Place a heap of cauliflower on each plate and top with 2–3 lamb cutlets. Arrange the roasted vegetables and caramelized olives on top of the cauliflower cream.

🦁 Comfort Cauliflower with Pancetta

Serves 2

Enjoy this classic pairing of cauliflower and cheese on its own or with some freshly smoked fish and lemon wedges.

CHEESE SAUCE
1¾ cups milk
2 bay leaves
4 black peppercorns
¼ nutmeg, freshly grated
1 white onion, peeled and halved
2 tablespoons butter
¼ cup all-purpose flour
½ cup good quality cheddar cheese, grated
½ teaspoon English mustard
½ teaspoon salt
½ teaspoon freshly ground black pepper

CAULIFLOWER
1 cauliflower, cut into bite-sized florets
2 tablespoons grapeseed oil
1 small white onion, peeled and finely chopped
2 cloves garlic, peeled and finely chopped
7 oz pancetta or free-range bacon in one piece, diced
2 teaspoons nigella seeds, toasted
2 teaspoons cumin seeds, toasted
grated Parmesan cheese, optional

1. Preheat the oven to 400°F/200°C.

2. To make the cheese sauce, combine the milk, bay leaves, peppercorns, nutmeg, and onion in a saucepan over low heat. Bring to just below a boil, stirring occasionally, then remove from the heat and set aside to infuse for 20 minutes.

3. Strain the mixture and discard the solids.

4. Heat the butter in a separate saucepan over low heat until just melted. Stir in the flour and gently cook, stirring, for 2 minutes until browned.

5. Slowly whisk in the infused milk to form a smooth sauce. Simmer over low heat for 5 minutes, then stir in the cheese and mustard. Any lumps can be removed by whisking with a hand whisk or stick blender, and set aside until the cauliflower is ready.

6. Cook the cauliflower in a saucepan with ¼ cup water until soft, but not mushy. Drain well and tip into a baking dish or shallow gratin dish.

7. Heat the oil in a frying pan and cook the onion and garlic until softened. Add the pancetta and cook until crisp.

8. Tip the onion, garlic, and pancetta into the dish with the cauliflower and mix well.

9. Pour the cheese sauce over the cauliflower. Sprinkle the nigella and cumin seeds, then the Parmesan, if using.

10. Bake for 25 minutes until golden brown and serve immediately.

Handmade Allspice Pasta with Walnuts and Fava Beans

Serves 4

Homemade pasta tastes so much better than store-bought and adding some freshly ground spices to the mix will give a new dimension of flavor, color, and texture.

PASTA
4 cups semolina flour
1 teaspoon salt
6 tablespoons freshly ground allspice berries
4 free-range eggs
water

SAUCE
1 tablespoon olive oil
1 red onion, peeled and finely chopped
4 cloves garlic, peeled and finely chopped
½ cup fresh walnuts, roughly crushed
½ cup chicken or vegetable stock
½ cup half & half
1 cup frozen fava beans, defrosted and peeled
zest and juice of 1 lemon
salt and pepper to taste
½ cup freshly shaved pecorino cheese to garnish
¼ cup fresh fennel tips to garnish

1. Combine the semolina flour, salt, and allspice in a large bowl. Make a well in the center. Drop in the eggs and mix well, adding a little water at a time. When the mixture starts to firm up, tip out onto a floured surface. Knead the dough thoroughly making sure all the ingredients are evenly distributed. Cover with plastic wrap and place in the refrigerator for several hours.

2. Remove the dough from the bowl. Divide into several pieces and work each through a pasta machine until the thinnest setting is reached.

3. Cut into 1½-inch wide strips and string up on a coat hanger or clothes horse to dry until required.

4. To cook the pasta, bring a large saucepan of cold water with 1 tablespoon each of salt and olive oil to a boil. Add the pasta, stirring occasionally. Cook for 3 minutes, drain well and add 2 more tablespoons of olive oil, to stop the pasta sticking together, and set aside.

5. To make the sauce while the pasta is cooking, heat the oil in a frying pan. Cook the onion and garlic for 2 minutes until soft and starting to brown. Add the walnuts and cook for 1–2 minutes or until the nuts are just browning. Add the stock and leave to reduce by half. This should take approximately 10 minutes. Reduce the heat to a simmer and stir in the half & half, allowing it to gradually come back to a simmer. Next, add the fava beans and stir well.

6. Add the pasta. Mix together well. Add lemon zest and juice. Taste to check seasonings and adjust as required.

7. Serve on a large platter topped with the pecorino and fennel tips.

🦁 St. Patrick's Day Corned Beef

Serves 4-6

Corned beef can make a delicious, cheap meal and is even better when the cooking liquid is infused with spices.

CORNED BEEF
4 lb 6 oz piece corned beef
1 large white onion, peeled and quartered
2 bay leaves
6 juniper berries
1 tablespoon black mustard seeds
4 whole cloves
2 tablespoons black peppercorns
2 tablespoons coriander seeds

1 bulb garlic

POTATO CAKE
8 large Yukon Gold potatoes
2 tablespoons butter
½ cup milk
1 tablespoon grapeseed oil
2 teaspoons salt
2 teaspoons freshly ground black peppercorns

SAUCE
¾ cup crème fraîche
2 tablespoons wholegrain mustard

7 oz fresh green beans, trimmed

1. To make the corned beef, place all the ingredients in a large saucepan filled with water to cover the meat and bring to a boil. Reduce the heat and simmer for 2 hours, skimming off the scum that collects on the surface from time to time.

2. Preheat the oven to 325°F/160°C.

3. Roast the garlic in a little olive oil for 10–15 minutes until soft and squishy. Set aside to cool until required.

4. To make the potato cake, peel the potatoes and cook until tender. Drain and mash until very smooth. Mix the butter and milk through the mashed potatoes. Squeeze out the garlic and mix through. Cover and set aside.

5. Once the corned beef is ready, lift it out of the pan and set it aside to rest for 5 minutes before slicing thinly.

6. Heat the oil in a large non-stick frying pan. Tip in the cooled mash, adding the salt and pepper and mixing well in the pan. Turn the mash as it browns – do this in slabs or sections. Cook until golden brown on both sides.

7. While the potato is browning, make the sauce. Combine the crème fraîche and mustard and mix well. Blanch the prepared green beans in boiling water for 2 minutes, then drain so they do not overcook. If you do this just prior to serving, the beans will still be warm.

8. To serve, place a slab of browned potato on each plate. Top with several slices of corned beef, the green beans, then spoon over some sauce.

❧ Mixed Spice Bread

Makes 1 loaf

This bread is best served in thick toasted slabs with glasses of mulled wine. Any leftovers make delicious French toast or bread pudding and the versatile mixed spice blend can be stored in an airtight container for up to 2 months.

MIXED SPICE BLEND
4 teaspoons coriander seeds
2 teaspoons ground cinnamon
1 piece cassia bark, approximately 1¼ x ¾ inch, finely ground
½ teaspoon ground nutmeg
½ teaspoon ground allspice
½ teaspoon ground ginger
¼ teaspoon whole cloves, finely ground
¼ teaspoon whole green cardamom seeds, finely ground

DOUGH
2 tablespoons active dry yeast
6 tablespoons warm water
3½ cups high-grade white flour
½ cup white sugar
4 teaspoons mixed spice blend
½ teaspoon salt
8 tablespoons cold butter
¼ cup candied citrus peel, chopped
⅔ cup currants or raisins
⅔ cup milk
finely grated zest and juice of 1 orange
1 egg, beaten

1. To make the mixed spice blend, combine all the ingredients and store in an airtight container until required.

2. To make the dough, place the yeast in a bowl, add the warm water and set aside to activate for 10 minutes.

3. Sift the flour into a large bowl and add the sugar, mixed spice blend, and the salt. Grate the cold butter into the dry ingredients and rub it in using your fingertips until the mixture resembles breadcrumbs.

4. Add the citrus peel, currants or raisins, and orange zest to the flour and mix well.

5. Heat the milk in a small saucepan until just warm. Add the yeast and water to the pan.

6. Make a well in the center of the flour and pour in the milk and yeast mixture. Stir in using your hand. Add the orange juice and the beaten egg. Still using your hands, mix to incorporate the wet ingredients.

7. Turn out on a floured surface and knead for 10 minutes or until the dough is smooth and no longer sticky. You may need to work in a little more flour.

8. Cover with plastic wrap and allow to rise for 2 hours in a warm place out of direct sunlight.

9. Preheat the oven to 350°F/180°C.

10. Grease a 9 x 5 x 3-inch loaf pan.

11. Tip out the dough and knead again for 5 minutes. Shape the dough and place it in the pan. Set aside, covered with plastic wrap, for 20 minutes in a warm place out of direct sunlight until doubled in size.

12. Bake for 1 hour and 10 minutes. Cover with a sheet of aluminum foil during the last 10–15 minutes if it is starting to look too dark. If you insert a knife into the center it should come out clean.

13. Remove from the oven and turn out immediately. Cool on a wire rack.

Baked Ricotta with Spiced Winter Fruits

Makes enough for 12

Traditionally winter comfort food, this dessert could also be enjoyed with summer berries. It is a great vehicle for other summer fruit, too, such as plums and apricots.

BAKED RICOTTA
1 lb ricotta
5 egg yolks
1¼ cups mascarpone or crème fraîche
¾ cup ground almonds
½ cup superfine sugar
1 vanilla pod, split and seeds removed

SPICED FRUIT
1 lb 7 oz apples, peeled, cored, and cut into eighths
1 lb 7 oz pears, peeled, cored, and cut into eighths
6 tablespoons honey
2 cinnamon sticks
4 star anise
¼ nutmeg, grated
3 tablespoons water
extra grated nutmeg to garnish (optional)

1. Preheat the oven to 325°F/160°C.

2. To make the baked ricotta, whisk together all the ingredients in a large bowl until smooth and creamy.

3. Pour into a greased 9 x 5 x 3-inch loaf pan and bake for 1 hour or until set.

4. Gently remove from the oven and set aside to cool before storing in the refrigerator overnight to set firmly.

5. To make the spiced fruit, place the prepared apples and pears in a frying pan with the honey, spices, and water. Gently cook over low heat for 5 minutes. Turn off the heat, cover and leave to steep and soften.

6. To serve, bring the baked ricotta to room temperature. Alternatively, it can be served warm straight from the oven. Gently turn out onto a large platter and spoon the fruits over the top. Sprinkle with the grated nutmeg if desired.

🦁 Ricotta Prune Tart

Serves 6

Ricotta is a versatile and relatively inexpensive ingredient that can vary quite a lot in flavor and texture. The more expensive brands are worth the extra money because they are wonderfully soft and milky, yet clean in flavor. Serve this tart cold with fresh berries in summer or with stewed fruit in winter.

PASTRY
2½ cups all-purpose flour
1 teaspoon baking powder
½ cup superfine sugar
11 tablespoons cold butter, cubed
2 free-range egg yolks

FILLING
½ cup pine nuts
⅓ cup prunes, pitted
⅓ cup Marsala
1 lb 2 oz ricotta cheese
2 free-range eggs
½ cup superfine sugar
finely grated zest of 3 lemons
½ nutmeg, freshly grated
3 allspice berries, freshly ground
extra egg yolk for glazing, beaten

1. Preheat the oven to 400°F/200°C.

2. Make the pastry first. Sift the flour, baking powder, and sugar together in a large bowl. Using your fingertips, rub in the butter until the flour mixture resembles breadcrumbs. Mix in the egg yolks to form a firm dough. Wrap loosely in plastic wrap and refrigerate for 45 minutes.

3. Dry-roast the pine nuts in the oven for 2–3 minutes until golden brown. Set aside to cool.

4. Place the prunes in a small bowl with the Marsala and soak for 20 minutes.

5. Push the ricotta through a sieve into a large bowl. Mix in the eggs, cooled pine nuts, prunes and Marsala, sugar and lemon zest. Mix well, then add the nutmeg and allspice.

6. Unwrap the pastry and divide in half. Roll out one half of the pastry on a floured surface to line the base and sides of a 10-inch well-greased flan pan. Carefully position the pastry in the flan pan and spoon in the ricotta mixture. Roll out the remaining dough and place on top, sealing the edges well with a wet finger. Brush the top with the beaten egg yolk. Bake for 40 minutes or until the top is crisp and golden. Remove from the oven and set aside to cool.

Deluxe Winter Espresso & Cardamom Mousse

Serves 6

For a dessert that can be put together in a few minutes this recipe can't be beat. Try a mix of dark and milk chocolates, but always use good quality.

    1 teaspoon green cardamom pods, crushed
    2 star anise
    1 teaspoon freshly roasted coffee beans
    1½ cups cream
    1 cup chocolate, 70% cocoa, cut into small pieces
    5 tablespoons unsalted butter, cubed
    2 free-range eggs at room temperature
    2 tablespoons runny honey

1. Add the spices and coffee beans to the cream and set aside to infuse in the refrigerator for at least 12 hours.

2. Place the chocolate and butter in a heatproof bowl. Position the bowl over a saucepan quarter-filled with water, ensuring that the water is not touching the bowl. Place the pan over medium heat until the chocolate and butter have softened and melted. Remove from the heat immediately.

3. Using a slotted spoon, lift out the spices from the cream and discard. Whip the cream until soft but not stiff.

4. Whisk the egg and honey together in a separate bowl until light and fluffy.

5. Gently add the cream and then the honey mixture to the chocolate and carefully fold together.

6. Pour into serving dishes. Cover and chill for at least 2 hours.

Dinner at the Yees'

Dinner with my family is always a rowdy affair. But silence usually descends once the food is placed on the table and everyone starts eating.

This chapter is all about real Chinese food with well-balanced flavors and is a tribute to my mother and grandfather who taught me many of their kitchen secrets.

A number of the dishes in this chapter can be cooked together to create a Chinese banquet that dinner guests will never forget.

🦁 Licorice Chicken and Bean-curd Parcels

Serves 2–3 as part of a Chinese feast

Dried bean-curd sheets are very useful to have in your pantry. They can be substituted for spring roll cases (once fried, they turn a lovely golden color) and are wonderful added to soups or stir-fries. Licorice needs to be stored in an airtight container away from other spices as it will taint the scent and taste of things around it.

MASTER STOCK
2⅛ cups water
3 star anise
5 licorice sticks
¾-inch piece of ginger
peel of 1 mandarin, dried
½ cinnamon stick
1 teaspoon Szechuan peppercorns
½ teaspoon fennel seeds
1 Chinese cardamom pod
½ teaspoon coriander seeds
½ cup white sugar

4 boneless free-range chicken thighs

BEAN-CURD PARCELS
2 large dried bean-curd sheets (approximately 12 x 20 inches)
1 spring onion, finely sliced
1 bunch onion bolts or 3 spring onions, roughly chopped
1 dried Chinese sausage, cut into long strips

finely chopped spring onions to garnish
black sesame seeds to garnish

1. Bring the water for the stock to a boil in a medium-sized saucepan. Place the next 9 ingredients on a piece of muslin and tie up the corners to form a bag. Add the sugar to the water and when it has completely dissolved, add the muslin bag to the pan. Simmer over low heat for 1 hour, then remove from the heat and allow to cool completely.

2. Submerge the chicken thighs in the cooled stock and allow to infuse overnight in the refrigerator.

3. To make the bean-curd parcels, preheat the oven to 350°F/180°C. Drain the chicken and discard the stock. Place the chicken on an oven tray and bake for 10–12 minutes or until just cooked. Remove and allow to cool.

4. Once the chicken is cool enough to handle, cut each thigh into 3–4 pieces.

5. Place the bean-curd sheets into a sinkful of warm water and allow the sheets to soften. Once softened, cut bean-curd sheets into smaller pieces that are easy to work with about 10 inches square.

6. Working with one sheet at a time, lay each sheet on the bench and place a piece of chicken in the middle. Top with a small quantity of spring onion, some onion bolts and, finally, some sausage. Carefully but tightly roll up the sheet to form a parcel. You can choose to leave the ends open rather than tucking them in if you prefer.

7. Choose an oven safe bowl that will fit inside a steamer, then layer the parcels in the bowl.

8. Steam over high heat until the water in the steamer comes to a boil. Reduce the heat and simmer for 12 minutes. Remove the bowl from the steamer and serve immediately garnished with the spring onion and a sprinkling of black sesame seeds.

🦁 *Firework Fish*

Serves 4 as part of a Chinese feast

Contrary to popular belief, Chinese food is not all about quick stir-frying and deep-frying. Many dishes involve up to three different cooking stages to ensure the flavors and textures of meats are exploited to the fullest; this dish is an excellent example of this.

FISH
2 x 1 lb hapuku steaks (or any other firm white-fleshed fish), skin on
6 tablespoons iodized salt
1 tablespoon *lapsang souchong* tea leaves

SAUCE
2 tablespoons grapeseed oil
2 cloves garlic, peeled and finely chopped
6 long, thin slices ginger root
2 Chinese eggplants (the long thin, purple variety), cut into thin diagonal slices
1 tablespoon black fermented and salted beans, washed well and rubbed to remove the skins and drained in several changes of water, then crushed to a paste
1 teaspoon sugar
1 teaspoon salt
4 tablespoons chicken or fish stock
1 spring onion, finely chopped
1 tablespoon arrowroot mixed to a paste with ¼ cup cold water

1. To prepare the fish, rinse the steaks and pat dry. Place in a non-metallic dish and sprinkle the salt over the fish, rubbing it in well to cover both sides of each piece. Cover and refrigerate for 30 minutes–1 hour.

2. Remove from the refrigerator and wash the fish to remove the salt. Pat dry.

3. Make a full pot of *lapsang souchong* tea and allow to steep for 3–5 minutes. Pour the tea into the bottom of a saucepan large enough to accommodate an oven safe bowl suitable for steaming. Place the fish in the bowl and fit it into the pan containing the hot tea. Cover and place over high heat. Once the tea is boiling, reduce the heat and allow it to steam for 10–12 minutes, depending on the thickness of the steaks. Remove the bowl from the saucepan and allow the fish to cool, first draining off any liquid that has accumulated in the bowl. Place a saucer or lid over the bowl to keep the fish warm. Discard the tea.

4. To make the sauce, heat the oil in a wok until very hot then add the garlic and ginger. Cook until lightly browned, then add the sliced eggplant. Turn to coat in the oil, then add the crushed beans, sugar, and salt and mix well. Pour in the stock and cover, reducing the heat to medium, and cook for 4–5 minutes until the eggplant has softened.

5. Remove the lid and mix again. Taste to check seasoning and add more sugar or salt as required. Stir in half the spring onion, then add the arrowroot paste mixing it in well.

6. Pour the eggplant sauce over the fish, garnish with the remaining spring onion and serve immediately on its own with steamed white rice or as part of a larger meal.

🐉 Fragrant Orange Pagoda Beef

Serves 4

Orange is an intense flavor that can easily railroad other more delicate flavors unless it is balanced carefully against them. The best way to achieve this is by counteracting it with something equally strong. In this recipe, chili is that opposing force.

peel of ½ an orange
2 teaspoons Szechuan peppercorns
½ teaspoon sugar
½ teaspoon salt
1 teaspoon cornstarch
12 oz lean beef, e.g. rump or sirloin, finely sliced
grapeseed oil for frying
3 cloves garlic, peeled and finely chopped
2 whole medium-heat red chilies, seeded and finely chopped
2 tablespoons peeled and julienned ginger root
1 teaspoon salt
1 teaspoon sugar
1 red pepper, seeded and finely sliced
1 bunch asparagus, sliced diagonally lengthwise
3½ oz snow peas, sliced into halves on the diagonal
1 spring onion, trimmed and sliced diagonally
1 bunch Chinese greens (ong choy or pak choy), woody ends discarded, sliced to same length
   as asparagus
4 tablespoons Chinese rice vinegar
2 tablespoons light soy sauce

1. Preheat the oven to 300°F/150°C.

2. Place the orange peel in a small baking dish and bake for 30 minutes or until dry and fragrant. Allow to cool slightly.

3. Toast the peppercorns in a dry frying pan for 40 seconds, being careful not to burn them, then place them in a mortar. Add the dried peel and grind well with the pestle.

4. Combine the sugar, salt, and cornstarch in a glass or ceramic bowl. Add the ground peel mixture, then stir in the sliced beef and mix well. Marinate for 30 minutes in the refrigerator.

5. Heat enough oil in a large frying pan to shallow-fry the beef. Once the oil is very hot, fry the beef in batches until crispy, draining each batch on paper towels as it is cooked, and adding more oil to the pan as required. It is very important to allow the extra oil to heat before adding the next batch of beef.

6. Heat 1 tablespoon of oil in a wok, then add the garlic, chili, ginger, salt, and sugar. Fry until the garlic is just beginning to brown. Add the remaining vegetables and stir-fry quickly, mixing them together as they cook.

7. Add the vinegar and soy sauce to the wok, then cover to allow the vegetables to steam for 1–2 minutes. Remove the lid, add the beef and mix well.

8. Serve immediately on a large platter with bowls of white steamed rice as part of a Chinese feast.

Drunken Chicken Salad

Serves 4 on its own or 6 as part of a Chinese feast

I have adapted this recipe from a classic Chinese dish, eliminating various steps to create a more straightforward version. Using a good quality Chinese wine is important as it will affect the flavor greatly.

MARINADE
1/3 cup salt
1/3 cup sugar
3 star anise
3 pieces dried mandarin peel
1½-inch piece ginger root, peeled and sliced
2 teaspoons Szechuan peppercorns
1 piece cassia bark, cut into ¾-inch cubes
1½ cups *shao-hsing* wine
6 cups water

3 lb 5 oz free-range chicken thighs, boned

DRESSING
1/3 cup vinegar
2 cups water
3 tablespoons sugar

SALAD
1¼ cups mung beans
2 spring onions, finely chopped
3½ oz snow peas, sliced finely
1 cup white Chinese turnip (also known as Japanese radish, daikon, Chinese radish, and Satsuma radish), grated
¼ cup toasted sesame seeds

1. To make the marinade, combine all the ingredients in a large saucepan and bring to a boil. Reduce the heat and simmer for 25 minutes. Turn off the heat and allow the liquid to cool completely. Submerge the chicken thighs in the cooled stock and allow to infuse overnight in the refrigerator.

2. To prepare the chicken, drain the chicken and discard the marinade. Place in a steamer that will fit tightly over a saucepan half-filled with cold water. Bring to a boil, then simmer for 25 minutes.

3. Allow to cool, then remove the chicken and shred the meat. Discard the steaming water and any liquid that may have accumulated around the chicken.

4. To make the dressing, combine the vinegar and water in a small saucepan, stirring in the sugar over a low heat until it dissolves. Allow to cool.

5. Pour the cooled dressing over the prepared salad vegetables and add the sesame seeds. Toss well. Add the shredded chicken and toss again.

6. Serve at room temperature as part of a Chinese meal or as a lunch dish.

🦁 Lotus Meets Fish

Makes 12 pieces

Available both dried and frozen, lotus root has a great texture and a sweet flavor with just a hint of woodiness. While tempura flour achieves a much lighter result, you could also use all-purpose flour. Whole dried shrimps are available only at Asian markets.

10 oz lotus root (dried or frozen)

FILLING
4 oz fresh white fish filets, e.g. tarakihi or gurnard
½-inch piece ginger root, peeled and roughly chopped
1 spring onion, roughly chopped
1 tablespoon light Chinese soy sauce
1 teaspoon sesame oil
1 tablespoon whole dried shrimps, soaked in hot water for 5 minutes, drained
1 serrano or habañero red chili, seeded and roughly chopped

BATTER
½ cup tempura flour
1 teaspoon salt
ice-cold water

grapeseed oil for deep-frying
2 tablespoons ground Szechuan peppercorns to garnish
2 tablespoons white sesame seeds to garnish
finely sliced spring onions to garnish

1. If using dried lotus root, soak it overnight in cold water to rehydrate, and if using frozen, defrost and drain well. Slice into thin rounds approximately ½ inch thick.

2. To make the filling, blend all the ingredients together in a food processor to form a paste. You may need to add a little water to achieve a smooth texture. Spread teaspoonfuls of paste onto the slices of lotus root and join them together to make little sandwiches.

3. To make the batter, mix the flour and salt together, then whisk in enough ice-cold water to form a thin batter that runs off the whisk easily.

4. Heat the oil in a frying pan.

5. Dip each sandwich in the batter, then fry in the oil until golden brown. You will need to turn them at least once throughout the cooking process to ensure a nice even color. Allow to drain on paper towels.

6. Mix together the ground pepper and sesame seeds and sprinkle over the sandwiches along with the spring onion. Serve hot or at room temperature with a bowl of light Chinese soy sauce for dipping.

🦁 Pork and Tofu Hot-pot Softie

Serves 4 as part of a Chinese feast

Soft tofu, as the name suggests, is much softer than regular tofu. It is used in most Asian countries to create thick soup-like dishes. Koreans do a fantastic version that is afire with chili and textured with seafood. This dish is best made in a small casserole dish or a traditional clay hot-pot, but a large ramekin with a saucer for a lid will be fine, too.

5 oz soft tofu
1 spring onion, finely chopped
2 teaspoons black sesame seeds
2 teaspoons sesame oil
2 eggs
5 oz ground pork
2 cloves garlic, peeled and finely chopped
2 tablespoons Chinese soy sauce
1 teaspoon salt
1 teaspoon sugar
2 teaspoons grapeseed oil
8 thin slices ginger root
1 mild red chili, seeded and finely sliced (or use a fiery dried or fresh chili if you prefer)
2 star anise
sliced spring onions to garnish
steamed white rice and stir-fried Chinese greens to serve

1. Place the whole block of tofu in the bottom of the casserole. Being very soft it may break up a bit. Sprinkle over the spring onion, sesame seeds, and sesame oil. Make 2 little wells in the tofu and crack an egg into each. Set aside.

2. Combine the ground pork with the garlic, soy, salt, and sugar in a bowl and mix well.

3. Heat the grapeseed oil in a wok until just beginning to smoke, then add the pork and remaining ingredients. Stir-fry for 3–4 minutes, stirring the pork to break it up as it cooks.

4. Once cooked, spoon the cooked pork over the tofu and cover. Place the oven safe dish over low heat (to avoid cracking the dish) then gradually increase heat to medium–hot. Cook for 15 minutes, just long enough to set the eggs, then garnish with spring onions and serve immediately with bowls of steamed white rice and stir-fried Chinese greens.

🦁 Mum's Most Wanted Pork Noodles

Serves 4

When I was a child, my grandfather used to send us large quantities of dried egg noodles from the other end of the country – good quality hand-made egg noodles were a rare thing indeed back in the 1970s and early '80s. Although this dish takes a little while to prepare, it is worth it.

1 heaped tablespoon dried, fermented, and salted black beans
4 tablespoons warm water
2 pork hocks, chopped (ask your butcher to do this)
½-inch piece ginger root, finely sliced
2 tablespoons thick dark Chinese soy sauce
1 teaspoon sugar
½ teaspoon salt
9 oz good quality fresh egg noodles
2 spring onions, finely sliced on the diagonal, or stir-fried Chinese greens to garnish

1. Soak the black beans in the warm water. Rinse well, discarding loose skins and sediment, then, using the back of a spoon, crush the beans to a lumpy paste.

2. Mix together the bean paste, chopped hocks, ginger, soy sauce, sugar, and salt and place in a saucepan with enough water to just cover the chopped hocks. Bring to a boil, then reduce to a simmer. Cook for 1 hour 20 minutes or until the meat is very tender and easily comes away from the bone. Remove from the heat and when cool enough to handle, remove the chopped hocks from the liquid and strip the meat from the bones. Return the shredded meat to the liquid and gently reheat, covered, to avoid the liquid reducing.

3. Boil the noodles in plenty of water, according to package instructions. Drain well but do not rinse. (Rinsing washes away a great deal of the flavor.)

4. Distribute noodles between 4 serving bowls. Spoon the shredded pork into the bowls, then ladle in the liquid, ensuring even distribution of the juice and pieces of ginger over the top.

5. Garnish with the spring onion or Chinese greens and serve immediately.

NOTE: If time is short, use spare ribs cut into small pieces to reduce the cooking time.

🦁 Stan's Five-spice Chicken with Noodles

Serves 6

My grandfather Stan would always cook this moist and juicy chicken dish, one of my favorites, when we visited. If you prefer, serve the chicken with rice and stir-fried vegetables.

FIVE-SPICE PASTE
2 whole star anise, ground
2½ teaspoons fennel seeds, ground
2 teaspoons cassia bark, ground
½ teaspoon Szechuan peppercorns, ground
4 tablespoons fermented brown beans, crushed to a firm paste
¼ teaspoon cloves, ground
2 teaspoons sugar
1 teaspoon salt
1½-inch piece ginger root, peeled and julienned
4 cloves garlic, peeled and finely chopped
3 tablespoons thin Chinese soy sauce

CHICKEN
3 lb 5 oz free-range whole chicken, cavity and body well washed and excess fat removed
2 spring onions, washed and finely chopped
2 cups boiling water
light soy sauce

NOODLES
6 bundles egg noodles, fresh or dried
2 tablespoons grapeseed oil
3 cloves garlic, peeled and finely chopped
1 teaspoon salt
2 bunches stalky Chinese greens (e.g. gai larn), trimmed and washed
2 spring onions, washed and sliced finely on the diagonal to garnish

1. To make the five-spice paste, blend all the ingredients together. Set aside.

2. Preheat the oven to 375°F/190°C.

3. Using several sheets of paper towels, pat the chicken dry then rub the prepared paste into the cavity of the chicken thoroughly. Any excess can sit inside the cavity. Add the spring onions.

4. Position the chicken to stand over a bowl so it looks like it is sitting upright and insert a funnel into the body cavity. Carefully pour in the boiling water a little at a time until it has filled the cavity completely. Remove the funnel and tightly sew the edges of the cavity together with a needle and thread so the water cannot escape, allowing the chicken to steam on the inside but roast on the outside. You can sew the neck end closed too if you like but I find that very little water is lost at this end.

5. Place two little ramekins filled with soy sauce on the bottom of the tray and rest the chicken on top. Rub the skin with a little soy sauce to help it brown then fill the bottom of the roasting tray with about ¾ inch of water. You need just enough to cover the bottom of the tray but not touch the chicken itself. Roast for 30–40 minutes or until the skin is well browned all over and the juices are running clean when a knife is inserted into the joint by the thigh.

6. Remove the cooked chicken from the oven and carefully cut through the stitches without damaging the surrounding skin. Drain the water into a bowl and reserve. This may take careful handling with at least one pair of tongs and both hands. Set the chicken aside to cool.

7. To cook the noodles, bring a large saucepan of cold water to a boil and add the noodles. Cook for 3–5 minutes if dried or 2 minutes if fresh. Drain the noodles and divide between 6 bowls.

8. Heat the oil in the same pan and add the garlic and salt. Cook for 1–2 minutes, then add the greens. Stir-fry for 2 minutes ensuring all the leaves are well coated with the oil. Ladle in a little of the reserved water, cover and steam for 2 minutes.

9. Spoon the greens into bowls, then quickly cut the chicken into bite-sized portions (including bones). Add to the bowls, sprinkle each with some spring onion and ladle in the chicken water to moisten the noodles.

10. Serve immediately.

NOTE: You can either use the delicious stock that has been created inside the chicken just as it is or thicken it a little by reducing it over high heat in a saucepan for a few minutes, adding a little cornstarch mixed with water. If you don't use all of it, refrigerate the rest for use in other stir-fries.

🦁 Rolled Sesame Balls

Makes 25–30 small balls

Simple and very tasty finger food, these can be served as an appetizer to an Asian-inspired dinner party or served with drinks.

4 medium fish filets, cut into 2-inch pieces (almost any fish is suitable)
5 spring onions, finely chopped
2 large shitake mushrooms, soaked in hot water for 10 minutes, squeezed dry and chopped
1½-inch piece ginger root, peeled and finely chopped
1 clove garlic, peeled and finely chopped
2 tablespoons Japanese soy sauce
juice of ½ lime
6 tablespoons sesame seeds
grapeseed oil for frying
Japanese soy sauce for dipping

1. Process the fish to a paste in a food processor. Add the next 6 ingredients and pulse to mix. Transfer the mixture to a bowl.

2. Using wet hands, roll the mixture into bite-sized balls. When finished, roll the ball in the sesame seeds to coat.

3. Heat enough oil in a deep frying pan to shallow-fry the balls. When the oil is smoking hot, drop in the balls, a few at a time to avoid crowding the pan, and cook for 3–4 minutes until they are browned. Drain on paper towels and serve with soy sauce.

✥ Simple Ginger Shrimp

Serves 4 as part of a Chinese feast

A quick dish that can be thrown together in a hurry and served with rice, this works just as well with chicken or finely sliced belly pork.

MARINADE
1½-inch piece ginger root, peeled and finely sliced
3 cloves garlic, peeled and finely chopped
2 tablespoons well washed and finely chopped cilantro root
2 tablespoons light Chinese soy sauce
1 teaspoon salt
1 teaspoon white sugar

1 lb raw shrimp, shelled and with tails and heads removed
2 tablespoons grapeseed oil
1 large bunch Chinese greens, such as gai larn or bok choy, well washed and any woody stems discarded, larger leaves and stems cut in half
2 tablespoons water
2 teaspoons arrowroot
2–3 teaspoons water
kaffir lime leaves to garnish

1. To make the marinade, combine all marinade ingredients in a bowl. Add shrimp and stir to coat. Marinate for up to 3 hours.

2. Heat the oil in a wok at a high temperature. Once hot and smoking lightly, add the marinated shrimp and move them about as they are stir-fried for 2–3 minutes. Once they are evenly colored but still a little undercooked, remove the shrimp from the wok and set aside. Leave the heat at a high temperature.

3. Add the greens to the wok and mix well with any remaining marinade in the wok. Add the water then cover and steam for 2–3 minutes or until just cooked – check every minute to avoid overcooking. Leave the heat at a high temperature.

4. Mix the arrowroot to a paste with the second measure of water. Return the shrimp to the wok along with any liquid that has accumulated, mixing well with the greens. Stir in the arrowroot paste, mixing well as you go to coat the shrimp and greens.

5. Bring back to a sizzle to ensure the shrimp are heated through, then tip out the mixture onto a large flat platter, arranging the shrimp and greens so they are equally distributed. Garnish with the lime leaves and serve immediately.

Peppered Mung Beans

Serves 4 as part of a Chinese feast

Make sure you use super-fresh mung bean sprouts – older ones will have a fermented taste to them that will spoil the dish.

1 tablespoon butter
2 cloves garlic, peeled and finely chopped
10½ oz fresh mung bean sprouts, washed and drained
1 tablespoon freshly ground black pepper
½ teaspoon ground white pepper
1 teaspoon salt
½ teaspoon sesame oil
1 teaspoon white sesame seeds

1. Heat the butter in a wok. When the butter starts to froth, add the garlic and allow it to brown slightly before adding the bean sprouts. Toss to coat with the butter, then add the seasonings. Cover and cook for 1–2 minutes until the sprouts have softened.

2. Drain off any water, then add the sesame oil and seeds, mixing well. Serve immediately.

Five-spiced Apricot Gems

Chinese people traditionally serve fresh fruit as a palate cleanser to finish a meal. Simplicity is the key. This is best made when apricots – or any other stone fruit you might choose – are at the height of their season.

2¼ cups superfine sugar
4 cups water
juice of 1 lemon
1 cinnamon stick
1 star anise
1 green cardamom pod
8 fennel seeds
5 Szechuan peppercorns
2 small apricots per person, kept whole with pits in
small mint leaves to garnish

1. Place the sugar and water in a saucepan over medium heat. Bring to a boil, stirring occasionally, until the sugar has dissolved. Add the lemon juice and spices and reduce the heat. When the mixture is down to a simmer, add the apricots and simmer for 45 minutes or until they are soft but still holding their shape.

2. Remove the apricots from the poaching syrup and allow to cool, reserving the syrup. Once cool enough to handle, peel off the skin and discard. Return the syrup to high heat and reduce until thick. Strain and discard the spices.

3. To serve, pour the syrup over the apricots and garnish with mint leaves.

Baked Treats

Although baking is a science requiring a careful hand and a good set of measuring equipment to get consistent results, it's also a very enjoyable and rewarding activity. Like most things in life, you get out of it what you put in so use quality ingredients wherever possible. The addition of spices can really transform baked treats into something truly heavenly.

Old-fashioned Cheese Sticks

Makes about 30

This dough is a fantastic base for different flavor variations. On those occasions when all you want is a classic cheese stick just leave out the spices and double the cheese! If you are in a hurry, don't worry about resting the dough – resting makes it a little lighter, but it is not essential.

15 tablespoons chilled butter, diced
2 cups all-purpose flour
2 eggs
2 teaspoons nigella seeds
1 teaspoon black mustard seeds
1 teaspoon coriander seeds, toasted and ground
1 teaspoon salt
½ teaspoon cayenne pepper
½ teaspoon fennel seeds, toasted
5–6 tablespoons water
1½ cups grated cheese, e.g. Parmesan, pecorino, Gruyère, or even just tasty cheddar

1. In a food processor, pulse the butter and flour until it turns to crumbs. With the motor running at a medium speed, add the eggs, one at a time, and process until a thick paste is formed. Add the spices and seasonings, followed by the water, one tablespoon at a time. When the dough has come together, remove from the processor. Wrap in plastic wrap and refrigerate for 1 hour.

2. Roll out the pastry to a thickness of approximately ¼ inch on a lightly floured surface. Sprinkle the cheese over the top, then fold the dough in half and then in half again. Squash flat to immerse the cheese inside. Allow to rest for 20 minutes before rolling out again to approximately ½ inch thick.

3. Preheat the oven to 345°F/175°C.

4. Cut into strips and give each a little twist before placing them on a baking tray. Bake for about 15 minutes or until crisp and golden brown.

5. Store in an airtight container and serve with chutneys, ham, gherkins, and pickles or on their own.

🦎 Olive Oil Wafers

Makes about 25–30 wafers if rolled thinly

These slightly sweet wafers go well with fruits and dessert dishes but also make a tasty change from savory crackers for a cheeseboard.

  2 tablespoons active dry yeast
  6 tablespoons warm water
  1 tablespoon sugar
  3½ cups all-purpose flour
  2 teaspoons anise seeds, toasted and finely ground
  2 teaspoons caraway seeds, toasted and finely ground
  2 teaspoons cumin seeds, toasted and finely ground
  1½ teaspoons salt
  finely grated zest of ½ lemon
  2 tablespoons sesame seeds, toasted
  3 tablespoons olive oil
  sea salt to sprinkle

1. Place the yeast in a large bowl and add the water, stirring to combine. Add the sugar and set aside to ferment for 5 minutes.

2. Add the flour, ground spices and salt, sesame seeds, and olive oil.

3. Mix well and then turn out on a floured surface. Knead for 10 minutes, adding more flour if necessary. Place in a large well-greased bowl and cover with plastic wrap. Set aside for 3 hours to rise in a non-drafty but warm place out of the sun.

4. Preheat the oven to 375°F/190°C.

5. Roll out the dough on a floured surface to ⅛ inch thick. Using a 1½-inch cookie cutter, cut out rounds. (If desired, use a smaller or larger cutter or cut freehand to get more rustic shapes.)

6. Place the wafers on a greased and floured baking tray and run the rolling pin over them one last time as they tend to puff up a little. Sprinkle each with a little sea salt then bake for 12–15 minutes or until they turn brown.

7. Store in an airtight container.

🦁 Ginger Ninja Bread

Makes 1 loaf

As a small child, my nephew was always a big fan of a thick slice of ginger cake. He and my mother were a great baking team, churning out treats with great gusto. It was he who gave this cake its name.

butter for greasing and flour for dusting
18 tablespoons butter
1 cup muscovado sugar
1 cup golden syrup, treacle, or molasses
1 vanilla bean
1 cup milk
2 teaspoons baking soda
2 eggs, beaten
3 cups all-purpose flour
2 teaspoons ground ginger
2 teaspoons ground cinnamon
1 whole nutmeg, freshly grated

TOPPING (optional)
3½ oz crystallized ginger cubes
9 oz mascarpone
finely grated zest of 1 lemon

1. Preheat the oven to 350°F/180°C.

2. Grease a 6 x 10-inch loaf pan. Line the base with parchment paper and dust the sides lightly with a little flour.

3. Melt the butter, sugar, and golden syrup in a saucepan over medium heat. Transfer to a large bowl and set aside to cool.

4. Cut open the vanilla bean and scrape out the seeds. Add the bean and seeds to the milk and gently heat until warm, not hot. Squeeze the bean to extract maximum flavor, then discard. Add the baking soda to the pan (don't be alarmed when it froths up), then stir in the beaten eggs. Pour into the bowl containing the cooled golden syrup and butter mixture. Fold in the sifted flour and the spices and mix together gently.

5. Bake in the center of the oven for 45 minutes or until a skewer inserted into the center comes out clean. Remove from the oven and allow to cool slightly in the pan before turning out onto a rack to cool.

6. To make the topping, if desired, mix ginger with the mascarpone. Add the lemon zest and mix well. Spread over the top of the cooled cake and serve immediately.

🦁 Date Marsala Buttermilk Cake

Lower in fat than ordinary milk, buttermilk is rich in calcium and makes for a moist cake with a longer shelf life. Use quality dried fruit – you will really notice the difference.

1 cup muscatels or plump raisins
½ cup dried apricots, roughly chopped
¾ cup boiling water
13 tablespoons unsalted butter
1½ cups muscovado sugar
3 large eggs
3 cups all-purpose flour
5 teaspoons baking powder
2 teaspoons baking soda
¼ nutmeg, freshly grated
6 cloves, toasted and finely ground
2 teaspoons caraway seeds, toasted and finely ground
2 teaspoons ground cinnamon
½ nutmeg, freshly grated
1¼ cups buttermilk (you may need a little more depending on how juicy your fruit is)

MARSALA ICING
7 tablespoons butter, softened
3 cups confectioners sugar, sifted to remove any lumps
¼ cup Marsala
9 oz mascarpone or cream, whipped

1. Preheat the oven to 345°F/175°C.

2. Lightly grease 2 x 9-inch round springform cake pans.

3. In a bowl, soak the muscatels and apricots in the boiling water for 5 minutes. Drain and mash with a fork until broken up but still chunky. Set aside.

4. Cream the butter and sugar until pale then add the eggs, one at a time, beating well after each addition. Sift the dry ingredients into the bowl and gently mix together before folding in the buttermilk and fruit.

5. Spoon the mix into the prepared cake pans and bake for 40–50 minutes or until the cakes have shrunk from the sides of the pans and a skewer inserted into the middle of the cake comes out clean.

6. Turn out the cakes onto a rack to cool before icing.

7. To make the icing, beat the butter until creamy. Slowly add the confectioners sugar and the Marsala, beating well after each addition.

8. Ice the top of each cake and allow to set for 30 minutes. Once set, spread a layer of mascarpone or cream on top of one of the cakes then sandwich the two together.

🦎 Chunky Pear Pecan Cake with Hard Cider Glaze

You can make this with apple, apricot, quince – anything that is in season and ripe. And if pecan nuts are unavailable, use fresh walnuts, brazil nuts, or even pine nuts.

butter for greasing tin
1½ cups vegetable oil
2 cups brown sugar
3 eggs
2 cups white flour or whole wheat flour
5 cloves, toasted and finely ground
2 teaspoons ground cinnamon
2 whole mace blades, toasted and finely ground
1½ teaspoons baking soda
½ teaspoon salt
1½ cups coarsely chopped pecan nuts
6 pears, peeled, cored and coarsely chopped
juice and zest of 1 lime

CIDER SYRUP
4 tablespoons butter
6 tablespoons brown sugar
2 tablespoons orange juice
6 tablespoons hard cider
2 tablespoons half & half

1. Preheat the oven to 335°F/165°C.

2. Grease a 10-inch round springform cake pan.

3. In a large bowl, beat together the vegetable oil and sugar until thick and cloudy.

4. Add the eggs, one at a time, beating well after each addition.

5. In a separate bowl sift together the dry ingredients. (If you are using whole wheat flour, do not sift it.) Mix well.

6. Stir in the egg and oil mix, then fold in the nuts, chopped pears, lime juice and zest, ensuring the fruit and nuts are evenly distributed.

7. Pour the mix into the prepared cake pan and bake in the center of the oven for 1 hour 15 minutes or until a skewer inserted into the middle of the cake comes out clean.

8. To make the syrup, melt the butter in a small saucepan and add the sugar, stirring constantly. Add the juice, hard cider, and half & half and stir well, allowing the mix to come to a boil before reducing the heat and cooking for a further 4 minutes.

9. Remove from the heat and allow to cool slightly before pouring over the warm cake. Serve immediately.

Super-fast Polenta Orange Cake

Makes 1 large cake

When you are pressed for time and you want a reliable recipe, this is it! The polenta provides texture as well as acting as a binding agent, and the result is a very moist cake that keeps well.

3 eggs, beaten
1 cup superfine sugar
1½ cups all-purpose flour, sifted
⅔ cup almond meal
½ teaspoon salt
2 teaspoons baking powder
¼ cup polenta
seeds from 3 green cardamom pods, toasted and finely ground
4 allspice berries, freshly grated or ground
1 cup olive oil
juice and grated zest of 3 oranges

1. Preheat the oven to 335°F/170°C.

2. Liberally oil an 11-inch round springform cake pan.

3. Beat the eggs with the sugar in a food processor. Add the flour, almond meal, salt, baking powder, polenta, and spices and process to blend. Slowly add in the olive oil and orange juice to form a thick paste. Add a little water if the mixture seems too dry or stiff – it should drop easily from a spoon. Add the zest and pulse the food processor to mix it in.

4. Spoon the batter into the prepared pan.

5. Bake for 50–60 minutes until well risen and slightly shrunken from the sides of the pan. You may need to cover the cake with aluminum foil for the last 10 minutes to stop it burning. Remove from the oven and allow to cool in the pan before turning out.

6. Serve on its own or with mascarpone mixed with 2 teaspoons of orange blossom water and garnished with fresh slices of orange.

Drink It In

A well-made drink can be just as satisfying as a beautifully cooked meal. In this chapter you'll find a variety of infusions suitable for serving at the start of a meal to set the mood for the culinary spice journey to follow. You might even be inspired to stock up your liquor cabinet so that you can whip up spice-infused cocktails any time.

Blossom Ball

Makes 1 bottle of infused vodka

Lychees are the stars of this divine drink that features a definite kick. Bear in mind that you'll need to infuse the vodka for at least a few days.

> 1 lb can peeled and pitted lychees
> 750 ml bottle good quality vodka, ¾ full
> seeds from 12 green cardamom pods
> 2 limes, sliced into thin segments
> soda water and fresh mint leaves to serve

1. Push the lychees into the bottle along with the cardamom seeds and lime segments.

2. Allow to infuse for at least 3 days but ideally a week. Keep out of direct sunlight and turn the bottle each day.

3. When ready to serve, pour the infused vodka into small glasses. Top up with a little soda water, add some ice and garnish with fresh mint leaves.

Summer Raspberry Vanilla Ratafia

Makes approximately 1.2–1.5 liters

The origin of the name "ratafia" is a little unclear, but a popular theory has it as a drink served to ratify an agreement or treaty. It is rather good on its own or on a hot day with a little soda and some mint leaves.

> 2 lb fresh raspberries
> 1 liter bottle good quality vodka or, better still, Havana Club white rum
> 750 ml bottle merlot
> superfine sugar
> vanilla pods
> skin from one orange with as little pith as possible, broken into several large pieces

1. Crush the raspberries with a potato masher then place in a covered container and refrigerate for three days, stirring daily.

2. Place the raspberries in a large fine sieve and allow to drain over a bowl for several hours. Measure the juice and add the same amount of vodka and the same amount again of merlot.

3. Weigh out the sugar. You will need ¼ cup of sugar for every 500 ml of liquid.

4. Stir until sugar has dissolved then pour into sterilized bottles, adding a vanilla pod to each and a strip of orange peel.

5. Allow to infuse for at least 2 months before drinking.

Sweet Hit

Makes 1 bottle of infused vodka or white rum

1 pint small, very ripe strawberries
½ teaspoon whole black peppercorns
750 ml bottle good quality vodka or white rum, ¾ full

1. Slice the strawberries in half and push them into the vodka bottle along with the peppercorns.
2. Shake and store in the freezer, turning the bottle every couple of days, until you can't wait any longer.
3. Strain and serve with fresh strawberries to garnish or use as a base for daiquiris.

Lamb's Wool

Makes 4–5 tall drinks

Dating from the 16th century, this drink combines crab-apples (or small tart cooking apples if crab-apples are unavailable) with spices and butter. It's wonderful on a cold night before a hearty feast.

8 crab apples or small tart cooking apples, cored but not peeled
about 25–30 whole cloves
2 tablespoons butter, cut into small cubes
4 cups / 1 liter pale ale
1 cup sugar or to taste
1 teaspoon ground ginger
3 cloves, extra
¼ whole nutmeg, freshly grated

1. Preheat the oven to 350°F/180°C.
2. Score the skin of each apple around the circumference (this will allow them to puff up in the oven rather than split open) and stud each with a few cloves.
3. Grease a small oven safe dish and place the apples in it. Dot each apple with some butter, then bake for 40 minutes or until soft. Remove from the oven to cool.
4. Scrape the flesh from five of the apples and discard the skin, core, and cloves, keeping the other three warm for the time being, and place in a saucepan with the ale, sugar, and ginger over low heat. Take care when adding the sugar as it will make the mixture froth suddenly. Whisk in the pan to combine and when it is hot (but not boiling), taste for sweetness, adding more sugar if necessary.
5. Pour the mixture into a large bowl and add the unpeeled reserved apples which are really just for show but can be eaten by a brave soul. Sprinkle in the grated nutmeg and serve immediately.

🦎 Red Pagoda

The unusual combination of liquorice and citrus makes for a refreshing drink in hot weather.

> 4–5 small pieces or 1 large piece liquorice bark
> 750 ml bottle good quality vodka, ¾ full
> 1 orange
> soda water and red grapefruit segments to serve

1. Push the liquorice bark into the vodka bottle.

2. Peel the orange and discard the flesh. Using a lighter, burn the edges of the peel carefully so they scorch and caramelize. Push the scorched pieces of peel into the vodka. (You may need to use a chopstick or skewer to get them right in.)

3. Allow to infuse for at least 3 weeks but ideally 6 weeks, turning the bottle from time to time.

4. Serve with ice and a little soda in tall glasses garnished with segments of grapefruit.

🦎 Winter Choco

Makes 1 bottle of infused vodka

Freshly roasted coffee can be used to great effect in cocktails. Ideally serve this little number in a shot glass to accompany a creamy dessert, or alongside a coffee at the end of a night of spicy feasting.

> 8 coffee beans
> 2 cinnamon sticks
> 2 vanilla pods
> 750 ml bottle good quality vodka, ¾ full

1. Put coffee beans, cinnamon sticks, and vanilla pods into the vodka bottle and leave to infuse for at least 3 months – the longer the better – turning the bottle from time to time.

2. Remove coffee beans and cinnamon but leave the vanilla pods.

3. Best served neat.

Kingly Condiments

Making chutneys or jams while fruit and vegetables are abundant and cheap means that even in the gloomiest of months, or when you are short of time, you can easily experience the joy of eating something you have created yourself. A delicious home-made spice-infused condiment can lift a fairly plain dish to a whole new level.

🏵 Pink Raisin Jam

Makes 3 x ½ pint jars

This quirky spread is excellent with meats and fish and its unusual color is bound to win comment. Unlike most other jams and chutneys, though, it has a relatively short life.

 ¼ teaspoon cumin seeds
 1 teaspoon fennel seeds
 5 fenugreek seeds
 4 tablespoons grapeseed oil
 ¼ teaspoon mustard seeds
 1½-inch piece ginger root, peeled and grated
 2 lb young rhubarb, well washed with any woody pieces removed, cut into ½-inch pieces
 1 apple, peeled, cored, and diced
 1 piece kokum
 1 teaspoon salt
 ¾ cup soft brown sugar
 ¼ cup raisins

1. Gently heat a dry pan and toast the cumin, fennel, and fenugreek seeds. This is best done one lot at a time to avoid the possibility of under-toasting or even burning them. Remove the spices and set aside.

2. Add the oil to the pan and heat. Add the mustard seeds and as soon as they begin to pop add the cumin, fennel, and fenugreek and coat well in the oil. Stir in the ginger and cook for 1 minute.

3. Add the rhubarb, apple, kokum, salt, and brown sugar and reduce the heat.

4. Remove the lid and add the raisins. Cook, uncovered, for a further 15 minutes to reduce and thicken, stirring occasionally to avoid sticking.

5. Pack into sterilized jars and store in the fridge for up to 2 weeks.

🏵 Aniseed and Fig Jam

Makes 1.5 liters

More of a compote than a jam, this condiment is delicious on bread or added to yogurt and other dairy products. It also makes an excellent treat served with muesli.

 2 cups water
 2 cups sugar
 juice and grated zest of 1 lemon
 1 cinnamon stick
 4 cups plump dried figs, chopped into chunks ¾ x ¾ inch
 2 teaspoons ground aniseed
 ½ nutmeg, freshly grated
 2 teaspoons rose water

1. Combine the water, sugar, lemon juice and zest, and the cinnamon stick in a large heavy-based saucepan and bring to a boil, stirring regularly. Reduce the heat and simmer for 5 minutes. Stir in the chopped dried figs and cook, still over low heat, for 15 minutes. Add the aniseed and nutmeg and cook for a further 5 minutes. Stir in the rose water, then take off the heat. Remove the cinnamon stick.

2. Pour into sterilized jars and seal. Store in a dark, cool place for at least 4 weeks before opening. The jam will keep for up to 2 years.

From left to right: Pink Raisin Jam, Aniseed and Fig Jam

Madras Feijoa Chutney

Makes 6–8 x 1 pint jars

This makes more spice blend than you need for this recipe, but it can be stored for up to 2 months and used to flavor chicken, fish and lamb curries or blended with yogurt to make a marinade. Make up the blend at least 1 day in advance to allow the flavors to infuse and mellow.

MADRAS SPICE BLEND

5 tablespoons coriander seeds
2 tablespoons cumin seeds
1 tablespoon yellow mustard seeds
1 teaspoon fenugreek seeds
seeds from 8 green cardamom pods
6 cloves
1 teaspoon amchur
1 dried Kashmiri or other medium-heat red chili
3 tablespoons ground turmeric
2 tablespoons ground ginger
1 teaspoon freshly ground black pepper
1 cinnamon stick

CHUTNEY

3 lb 5 oz feijoas, flesh spooned out of the skins and roughly chopped
2 lb 3 oz onions, peeled and sliced
2 cups brown sugar
½ cup crystallized ginger, chopped
4 cups white wine vinegar
3 tablespoons madras spice blend
2 tablespoons salt

1. To make the spice blend, toast the seeds in a dry frying pan until they just begin to turn brown. They will continue to cook even after you take them off the heat.

2. Allow to cool, then grind to a fine powder with the other whole spices. Add the previously ground spices and mix together well. Transfer to an airtight jar until required.

3. To make the chutney, combine the feijoas and onion in a large saucepan and cook for 10 minutes over moderate heat to soften. Add the brown sugar, ginger, vinegar, spice blend, and salt.

4. Reduce the heat and simmer for 1½ hours, stirring occasionally to stop the mixture sticking.

5. Pack into sterilized jars and leave for at least 1 week.

🦁 Slow Mango and Clove Chutney

Makes 4-6 x 1 pint jars

Maybe it is the Indian ability to assimilate that has led to so many of their wonderful culinary ideas becoming mainstream. Mango chutney has to be a great example of this and I highly recommend my particular version with kedgeree or slabs of home-baked ham.

    5 whole cloves
    10 black peppercorns
    1 dried Kashmiri or other medium-heat red chili
    3 red onions, peeled and finely chopped
    1¾ cups white wine or cider vinegar
    2 bay leaves
    1 teaspoon black mustard seeds
    2 teaspoons cumin seeds
    5 mangoes, peeled, pitted, sliced into wedges
    4 cooking apples, peeled and finely chopped
    2 cups sugar
    1 teaspoon ground ginger
    10 allspice berries
    2 leafy curry leaf stems, leaves stripped, washed and reserved

1. Combine the cloves, peppercorns, and chili in a muslin spice bag and secure the top with string.

2. Place the spice bag in a large saucepan with the onion, vinegar, and bay leaves and simmer over medium heat for 10 minutes or until the onion has softened. Remove from the heat and set aside.

3. Toast the mustard seeds in another large saucepan until they begin to pop, then transfer to a dish. Toast the cumin seeds in the same saucepan until they brown slightly (20 seconds), then add the chopped mango and apple. Stir in the mustard seeds and cook for 15 minutes or until the fruit has softened.

4. Add the sugar, ginger, allspice, and curry leaves and simmer, almost at a boil, until the mixture thickens.

5. Add the onion mixture to the pan and cook for 40 minutes, covered, stirring occasionally to avoid any sticking. Remove the lid and cook for 1 hour at a low heat until the chutney has reduced but is still able to be ladled or poured into the jars.

6. Pack into sterilized jars and seal. Store in a dark cupboard for at least 3 months.

🦁 Red Cumin Mayonnaise

Makes enough for 1 serving

Although not really a mayonnaise given that potato is the main ingredient, this is delicious with seafood and fish dishes or drizzled over salads. It will only keep for a few days so serve generously.

    9 oz floury potatoes, peeled and quartered
    5 cloves garlic, peeled and finely chopped
    10 saffron threads
    2 small ancho or chipotle chilies, seeded and finely chopped
    2 red peppers, roasted, seeded, and skins removed
    juice of ½ lemon
    1 tablespoon whole cumin seeds, toasted and finely ground
    1 teaspoon salt
    ½ teaspoon freshly ground black pepper
    1 cup olive oil

1. Place the potatoes in a large saucepan and add enough water to just cover. Add the garlic, saffron, and chilies. Cook, uncovered, over medium heat until the water has almost evaporated and the potatoes are soft.

2. Transfer the contents of the pan to a food processor and add the peppers, lemon juice, cumin, salt, and pepper and process to mix. With the motor running, slowly drizzle in the olive oil. Taste to check seasonings and adjust as required.

3. Spoon the mixture into a dish and serve with battered shrimp, grilled chicken, or roasted vegetables.

🦁 Orange and Ginger Chutney

Makes 4–6 x 1 pint jars

Great served with fish, chicken, and meats, this delicious and easy chutney is best made when oranges are in season and have lots of juice.

    4 oranges, peeled and sliced into ¾-inch chunks
    2 apples, peeled and sliced into ¾-inch chunks
    1 onion, peeled and sliced finely into long slivers
    3-inch piece ginger root, peeled and finely sliced
    1 tablespoon salt
    1 tablespoon black mustard seeds
    2 cups cider vinegar
    1 cup brown sugar

1. Place all the ingredients in a large heavy-based saucepan and simmer for 1½ hours until thickened.

2. Taste to check seasonings and adjust as required. Add more orange juice if you want a lighter flavor or a just a bit of extra vinegar to give it more tang, in which case you will need to allow the mixture to simmer for a further 10 minutes.

3. Pack into sterilized jars and store for at least 3 weeks.

Clockwise from top: Slow Mango and Clove Chutney (recipe page 175);
Orange and Ginger Chutney; Patient Date and Lemon Chutney (recipe page 178)

🦎 Patient Date and Lemon Chutney

Makes enough for 3-4 x1 pint jars

You'll need lots of patience before sampling this chutney, but once you've tasted it, it's bound to become a permanent fixture on your table and it's great added to stews by the spoonful or mixed with a little oil to make a simple marinade or vinaigrette.

> zest and flesh of 6 lemons, pith removed, finely chopped
> juice of 4 lemons
> 2 tablespoons salt
> 8 oz dates, pitted
> 2 bay leaves
> 6 cloves garlic, peeled and roughly chopped
> 1½-inch piece ginger root, peeled and finely grated
> 1 cinnamon stick
> 2 tablespoons seeds from cardamom pods, finely ground
> 4 whole star anise
> ½ cup white wine vinegar or verjuice
> 8 oz brown sugar

1. Combine the lemon zest, flesh, and any juice with the salt and leave for 4 hours in a ceramic bowl. The acid of lemons may react with a metal bowl and leave an odd taste to your chutney.

2. In the meantime, chop the dates into small pieces. Soak them in a little warm water, then drain well and set aside.

3. When the lemon mixture is ready, transfer it to a heavy-based saucepan and add the bay leaves, garlic, ginger, cinnamon, cardamom, star anise, and vinegar and bring to a boil. Reduce the heat and simmer for 5 minutes.

4. Add the sugar and the chopped dates and stir well to combine. Simmer for 1 hour, stirring occasionally to avoid sticking or burning. The chutney should be thick and reduced.

5. Remove the star anise and cinnamon quill before packing the mixture into sterilized jars and sealing.

6. Store in a dark place for 6 weeks or longer, if you can hold out, to mature.

NOTE: Dried dates will make this chutney more economical though fresh dates will produce the best result.

Yellow Ginger Pickle

Makes enough for one good-sized bowl to serve with a meal

This sublime pickle can feature as an accompaniment to an Indian feast, alongside roasted or barbecued meats, in sandwiches or with sausages.

> 2-inch piece of ginger root, as fresh and tender as possible
> 2 tablespoons vegetable oil
> 3 leafy curry leaf stems, leaves stripped, washed and reserved
> 2 teaspoons black mustard seeds
> 1 tablespoon yellow lentils, well washed and soaked in several changes of cold water for 3 hours
> 1 oz block tamarind, soaked in ½ cup hot water for 30 minutes, then strained
> 1 lemon, cut into quarters
> 1 teaspoon sugar
> 4 green Thai chilies, seeded and cut in half lengthwise
> salt to taste

1. Cut the piece of ginger in half lengthwise if necessary, then finely slice into bite-size slivers. Set aside.

2. Heat the oil in a large frying pan, then add the curry leaves and mustard seeds. Carefully shake the pan over the heat until the seeds begin to pop. Add the yellow lentils and mix well to coat with oil. Cook for 25 minutes until the lentils begin to brown, then add the sliced ginger, mixing well to combine.

3. Reduce the heat and add the tamarind water, quartered lemon, sugar, and chilies, stirring well.

4. Cook for a further 15–20 minutes or until the lentils and ginger have begun to break down and soften and the tamarind water has evaporated. Taste and salt as needed.

5. Allow to cool before removing and discarding lemon quarters.

6. Store, covered, in the fridge for up to 1 week.

NOTE: This is best made when fresh ginger comes into season, not just because there is no need to peel fresh ginger when it's young and tender but also because of its superb flavor and fragrance.

Appendices

&

Index

✳ Weights and Measures

The following amounts have been rounded up or down for convenience.
All have been kitchen tested.

METRIC	IMPERIAL	METRIC	IMPERIAL
10–15 g	½ oz	50–55 ml	2 fl oz
20 g	¾ oz	75 ml	3 fl oz
30 g	1 oz	100 ml	3½ fl oz
40 g	1½ oz	120 ml	4 fl oz
50–60 g	2 oz	150 ml	5 fl oz
75–85 g	3 oz	170 ml	6 fl oz
100 g	3½ oz	200 ml	7 fl oz
125 g	4 oz	225 ml	8 fl oz
150 g	5 oz	250 ml	8½ fl oz
175 g	6 oz	300 ml	10 fl oz
200 g	7 oz	400 ml	13 fl oz
225 g	8 oz	500 ml	17 fl oz
250 g	9 oz	600 ml	20 fl oz
300 g	10½ oz	750 ml	25 fl oz
350 g	12 oz	1 liter	34 fl oz
400 g	14 oz		
450 g	1 lb		
500 g	1 lb 2 oz		
600 g	1 lb 5 oz		
750 g	1 lb 10 oz		
1 kg	2 lb 3 oz		

Please note:
a pint in the UK is 16 fl oz
a pint in the USA is 20 fl oz

BAKING PAN SIZES

Common square and rectangular baking pan sizes:

20 x 20 cm	8 x 8 inch
23 x 23 cm	9 x 9 inch
23 x 13 cm	9 x 5 inch loaf pan

Common round baking pan sizes:

20 cm	8 inch
23 cm	9 inch
25 cm	10 inch

OVEN TEMPERATURES

Celsius	Fahrenheit
120°	250°
150°	300°
160°	325°
180°	350°
190°	375°
200°	400°
220°	425°

ABBREVIATIONS

g	gram
kg	kilogram
mm	millimeter
cm	centimeter
ml	milliliter
°C	degrees Celsius

Note also: baking paper = non-stick parchment paper.
In New Zealand, South Africa, the UK, and the USA 1 tablespoon equals 15 ml.
In Australia 1 tablespoon equals 20 ml.

❧ Spice Glossary

The following notes are intended to help you understand more about the spices you are most likely to use in your cooking.

AJOWAN
A native to India, ajowan also grows in Afghanistan, Egypt, Pakistan, and Iran where it is incorporated regularly into potato and rice dishes. It is a member of the pungent flavor group and the seeds have a taste not unlike thyme with a peppery note and long aftertaste. Used in breads and savory baking, it also complements vegetables from the cabbage family. Its small size means it can be added to dishes whole rather than toasted.
Use: with chili, coriander seeds, cumin seeds, and paprika.
Look for: seeds that are uniform in color with no stems.
Store: in an airtight container away from the light and heat. Seeds will keep for up to 2 years.

ALLSPICE
A native to Jamaica, the dried unripe allspice berry is used in many different cuisines in sweet cakes and cookies, marinades, pickles, and pâtés. A member of the pungent flavor group, it works very well with shellfish and meats and is best purchased whole rather than ground as ground allspice quickly loses its flavor.
Use: with bay leaves, turmeric, paprika, ginger, fennel seeds, cumin seeds, coriander seeds, cloves, and cinnamon.
Look for: whole dried berries (do not be concerned by difference in size of berries as this does not affect flavor).
Store: up to 3 years away from heat and light.

AMCHUR
Amchur is the dried unripe fruit of the mango tree, which grows very well in subtropical areas. The powdered form with its slightly greenish-yellow hue is the most widely available. With its acidic and fruity scent, amchur is a natural souring agent and is used in marinades to tenderize meats, and in chutneys and pickles to add a sharp edge. Part of the tangy flavor group.
Use: with ginger, pepper, chili, coriander, cumin seeds, and star anise.
Look for: small quantities in ground form.
Store: away from heat, light, and any humidity and use within 1 year.

ANISEED
Native to the Middle East, aniseed – with its distinctive licorice flavor – is used in many traditional dishes, often to balance heavy meaty flavors. A member of the sweet flavor group, aniseed has also long been used in cakes and cookies. Like many other spices, it is best purchased whole then ground when required but as it is not readily available in whole form, buy small quantities of ground.
Use: with allspice, cloves, dill, and fennel.
Look for: even color and a strong scent.
Store: in a cool, dry cupboard for up to 1 year.

BAY LEAVES
More of a herb than a spice, the leaves of this well-known evergreen native to Asia Minor is a staple in French cooking and is used in everything from stocks and sauces, pâtés and terrines, to fish dishes and soups. Always buy whole leaves rather than powder as recipes usually call for leaves to be added whole and removed prior to serving. Part of the pungent flavor group.
Use: with other herbs (such as basil, oregano, and rosemary), paprika and in many traditional spice blends.
Look for: leaves that are dark green in color with no appearance of yellowing.
Store: whole for up to 3 years.

BLACK LIMES
Originally from South-east Asia, black limes are made by boiling fresh limes in salt then drying them. They have a fermented, sweet but acidic flavor. Also used in Middle Eastern cooking, the black lime, a member of the tangy flavor group, works as a natural tenderizer for meats but also adds a special fragrant element to casseroles and stews, particularly fish stews.
Use: with paprika, allspice, cloves, coriander seeds, and turmeric.
Look for: dried limes that have no signs of mold.
Store: away from light and humidity for up to 2 years.

BROWN CARDAMOM
Not to be confused with green cardamom, the brown variety, native to India, is – unsurprisingly – dark brown in color with a thick, woody outer case that must be crushed to access the soft and sticky seeds within. Part of the pungent flavor group, brown cardamom was in the past often wrongly identified as a second-rate green cardamom. Whole cardamoms are dried out above a fire, which gives the seeds their lovely smoky flavor. Unlike green cardamom, the brown seeds do not require toasting prior to use as they are soft and easily blended. A great addition to barbecue marinades, Asian master stocks, and Indian spice pastes.
Use: with turmeric, star anise, and green cardamom. Also good blended with Spanish paprika to intensify the smokiness and chili, allspice, coriander, and cumin seeds.
Look for: whole, unbroken pods.
Store: in a cool, dry place for up to 3 months in seed form or up to 2 years in pod form.

BROWN CHINESE CARDAMOM
Similar in appearance to regular brown cardamom, brown Chinese cardomom can easily be mistaken for the former. However, this Chinese variety has an astringent scent and a camphor-like flavor. Ideal in soups, this particular cardamom tends not to be used in many dishes besides Chinese master stocks but do experiment with it as the seeds work beautifully in marinades for chicken and pork.
Use: with coriander seeds, fennel seeds, star anise, and Szechuan pepper.
Look for: unbroken pods with no splits.
Store: well sealed for up to 2 years.

CARAWAY
A member of the pungent flavor group, caraway, with its distinctive warm flavor (almost like a meeting of fennel, anise, and orange peel, followed by a minty aftertaste), has been used for both medicinal and culinary purposes for 3,000 years. It's a plant that thrives in most climates but today Holland is the largest producer. It works well with pork as with cabbage. Caraway is an ingredient in spice blends such as harissa and garam masala.

183

Use: with cumin seeds, coriander seeds, allspice, fennel seeds, turmeric, paprika, and ginger.
Look for: seed form rather than ground.
Store: well sealed in small quantities for up to 2 years.

CASSIA

Native to China, cassia is often confused with cinnamon due to its similarity in flavor and appearance. Cassia is available to buy as either whole pieces of bark or rolled sticks (much thicker than those of its cinnamon cousin). It can also be bought in ground form and can be distinguished from cinnamon by its much redder color. Cassia is often used by commercial bakers as it has a much stronger aroma and taste than cinnamon.
Use: with allspice, caraway, cardamom, chili, coriander, cumin seeds, ginger, liquorice, nutmeg, star anise, tamarind, and turmeric.
Look for: clean-looking bark with no mold. Even color in ground form.
Store: in ground form for up to 6 months and whole in an airtight container for up to 3 years.

CHILI

The chili comes in many shapes and forms. It is part of the hot flavor group and the difference between a fresh chili and a dried chili can make a huge difference. A dried chili will add a caramelized yet fruity and smoky flavor that can greatly enhance a good meat marinade or sauce, while a fresh chili has the bright spark of heat, intensity of flavor and sweetness that is so easily recognizable in many Thai dishes. Chilies can be bought whole and fresh as well as whole and dried, flaked and powdered. Listed below are some of the more common types of chili complete with a hotness (or piquancy) rating as defined by the Scoville Scale. To give you an idea of how the Scoville Scale works, a red or green sweet pepper has a Scoville rating of zero (no heat detectable) whereas a habañero chili (one of the hottest chilies available), has a heat rating of 10+.

- ❀ Anaheim – elongated, mild chili, often used in sauces and stews with a heat level of 2.
- ❀ Ancho – large dried chili used regularly in Mexican dishes. Mild with sweet tones of coffee and raisin and a little woody smokiness, it has a heat level of 4.
- ❀ Bird's eye – a very small and hot chili commonly used in Thai cuisine with a heat level of 9.
- ❀ Cayenne pepper – a blend of chilies with a consistent heat level of 8. Often used to replicate whole dried chilies in a more convenient powdered form.
- ❀ Chili flakes – dried Indian chilies that have been broken down into flakes to create a heat level of 7. Often used in Italian dishes to give a smoky, woody flavor.
- ❀ Chili powder – a wide variety of powders are available that can range in heat level. An orange color indicates a milder heat and a redder tinge suggests a more intense heat.
- ❀ Chipotle – a jalapeño chili that has been smoked to give it a very distinct flavor. Used most often in Mexican soups and stews, it has a heat level of 5.
- ❀ Habañero – hottest of the hot with a 10+ level of heat, this chili has a sweet flavor with fruity elements. It's best to use whole for flavor, then remove it from the dish prior to eating.
- ❀ Kashmiri – now readily available, these Indian chilies are often found in powdered form and are a bright red color with a heat level of 7.

- ❀ Pasilla – Mexican chilies, also known as chilaca, are fairly large in size and relatively mild. Essential in moles, they have a lovely molasses-like flavor.
- ❀ Poblano – bell-shaped chilies often used for stuffing with other ingredients with a heat level of 4–6.
- ❀ Serrano – small tapered chilies, ideal in salads and salsas with a heat level of 5–7.
- ❀ Thai chili – ranging from green to red. Can vary in heat but are generally perfect for slicing and adding to stir-fries for a medium heat or for slipping whole into soups or stocks for a milder infusion.

Store: keep dried and ground chili well away from humidity to avoid mold for up to 3 years. Flaked chilies tend to deteriorate faster so buy smaller quantities and keep away from heat, light and moisture. Fresh will last in the refrigerator for up to 3 weeks.

CINNAMON

Cinnamon, a native of Sri Lanka was once used for embalming by the ancient Egyptians. Cinnamon comes from bark stripped from the tropical laurel tree and rolled into "sticks" up to 3 feet in length, which is then left to dry. It can be bought ground or in short sticks. It is used in both sweet and savory dishes.
Use: with allspice, caraway, cardamom, chili, coriander, cumin seeds, ginger, liquorice, nutmeg, star anise, tamarind, and turmeric.
Look for: clean-looking sticks. Even color in ground form.
Store: whole in airtight containers for up to 3 years. Ground cinnamon should be used within 6 months.

CLOVES

Cloves appear in the spice blends of the Middle East, Europe, and Asia. With their distinctive smell, cloves are part of the pungent flavor group and are native to the Molucca islands, east of Indonesia. Cloves were used as an early form of breath freshener as well as a way (unsuccessful as it happens) to ward off the plague back in the 13th century. Ground cloves will lose their oils quickly so buy in small amounts and use as soon as possible.
Use: with allspice, amchur, green cardamom, chili, coriander seeds, cumin seeds, kokum, liquorice, nutmeg, star anise, tamarind, and turmeric.
Look for: whole cloves of an even dark-brown color.
Store: for up to 2 years in a dry, cool cupboard.

CORIANDER SEEDS

One of the most common spices, coriander seeds have a warm and woody tone that goes with almost anything. A hearty native of southern Europe and the Middle East, in ancient times it was used to make love potions and has even been found in the tombs of the Pharaohs. Ground seeds lose flavor quite quickly so use within 9 months.
Use: with allspice, cinnamon, chili, cumin seed, fennel seed, ginger, green cardamom, and pepper.
Look for: seeds free from stalks of an even brown colour.
Store: for up to 2 years in a dry, cool cupboard.

CUMIN SEEDS

Cumin grows wild in the Middle East where it has flourished for centuries. Referenced in the Bible and regarded by the Romans as a symbol of greed, cumin was used for its ease of blending with other flavors and spices. A member of the pungent flavor group, it can be found in classic spice blends of the Middle East. Ground seeds will lose their flavor fast so buy small quantities and use within 9 months.

Use: with allspice, chili, cinnamon, cloves, coriander seeds, green cardamom, nigella, paprika, tamarind, and turmeric.
Look for: evenly colored seeds with no dust or grit.
Store: for up to 2 years in a dry, cool cupboard.

DILL SEEDS

Often confused with caraway, dill seeds taste similar to the former but look like a small version of the fennel seed. Belonging to the pungent flavor group, they are commonly found in both Scandinavian and Russian cuisines. Dill seeds were given to Roman gladiators as a symbol of vitality and in later years they were also thought to ward off evil during the Middle Ages. These days they are acknowledged as an effective aid to digestion. Try them with fish and add it to pickles and breads.
Use: with allspice, chili, cinnamon, coriander seeds, cloves, fennel seeds, ginger, mustard seeds, and pepper.
Look for: even color, free of dust stalks and grit.
Store: seeds in a cool, dry cupboard for up to 3 years.

FENNEL SEEDS

The digestive powers of fennel with its strong aniseed flavor have long been acknowledged, especially back in ancient times by the Chinese, the Egyptians, and the peoples of India. Native to southern Europe, fennel grows just about anywhere. Fennel seeds are part of the amalgamating flavor group and are used in sauces, curries, marinades, and in Italian-style sausages. Versatile fennel combines well with most spices in sweet and savory dishes.
Use: with allspice, cardamom, chili, cinnamon, cumin, galangal, paprika, tamarind, and turmeric.
Look for: seeds that are an even green color. Watch out for foreign matter such as small stones.
Store: in a cool, dry cupboard for up to 3 years.

FENUGREEK SEEDS

Often found in Indian cuisine, fenugreek was used long ago to entice reluctant cattle to eat hay, and along with cinnamon it was cultivated by the Egyptians for embalming purposes. A member of the pungent flavor group, it has a bitter flavor that mostly disappears on toasting, a process that enhances the nutty, slightly burnt sugar flavor. Include it in curry spice blends and other savory applications, but use sparingly. When ground, the seeds will lose flavor and aroma quickly.
Use: with cumin and coriander seeds, mustard seeds, nigella, pepper, turmeric, cloves, and cinnamon.
Look for: even golden-colored seeds. Watch out for foreign matter such as small stones.
Store: whole seeds for up to 3 years.

GALANGAL

Native to Java and a member of the ginger family, galangal, which belongs to the pungent flavor group, is hot and clean in taste. It is very hard to get fresh but is readily available dried in slices or frozen in pieces. Used extensively in Thai cooking in which it works to neutralize overly fishy flavors in curries and soups, it also features in curry pastes, sambals, and stir-fries.
Use: with allspice, chili, cinnamon, cloves, coriander, cumin seeds, mustard, nigella, paprika, pepper, and turmeric.
Look for: frozen pieces or dried in slices.
Store: ground in a cool, dry cupboard for up to 1 year.

GINGER

Used fresh and processed to create crystallized and preserved ginger as well as powdered, its exact origins are a little sketchy but it is thought to have first been used in East Asia. The first gingerbread was said to have been made near Greece in 2400 BC, suggesting that trade of ginger was already in place. It is a member of the pungent flavor group, and is used in a huge array of sweet and savory dishes around the world including stocks and soups, cookies and cakes and spice blends of Asia and the Middle East. Fresh ginger is readily available while its ground form is much more subtle, working well in cakes and cookies. Grate fresh with a very sharp grater to break and release the juices.
Use: with turmeric, allspice, cinnamon and cassia, chilli, cloves, coriander and cumin seeds, fennel seeds, paprika and star anise.
Look for: ground: even-colored with a strong aroma, not too coarse; fresh: plump pieces
Store: ground ginger must be stored in dark dry conditions for up to 6 months; whole dried ginger will last a little longer in the same conditions.

GREEN CARDAMOM

A member of the pungent flavor group and native to the south of India and Sri Lanka, cardamom has long been cultivated for its distinctive liquorice taste and breath-freshening properties. Today, however, it is used throughout the world in pastes and blends, in coffee, sweets and fruit dishes, and baked rice and milk puddings. Its woody casing keeps the seeds rich in oils so buy this spice whole, then crush the casing to release the seeds.
Use: with cinnamon, caraway, cumin and coriander seeds, fennel, ginger, star anise, all peppers, and turmeric.
Look for: uncracked pods that are an even bright lime green in color.
Store: for up to 3 months in seed form or whole pods for up to 2 years in a cool, dry place.

JUNIPER

A refreshing pine flavor with a sweet, slightly acidic scent would best describe this member of the pungent flavor group which grows in many different parts of the world including the Himalayas, North America, Norway, and the Mediterranean. Used to flavor gin, juniper is also great teamed with wild game, added to sauces for meats and casseroles and as a flavorsome addition to terrines and pâtés. Juniper branches were traditionally burned to refresh the air in stale rooms during winter in Switzerland. The crushing of berries should be done just before they are needed as once the oils are exposed to the air, they quickly evaporate.
Use: with herbs (such as oregano, parsley, sage, and thyme) rather than spices but it does work well with paprika.
Look for: large plump berries that show no signs of mold.
Store: whole berries away from heat, light, and moisture for up to 3 years.

KOKUM

Belonging to the tangy flavor group, this dried rind of a plum-like fruit from a tropical tree is found only in certain regions of India and has an astringent, but pleasantly fruity, taste. As the rind is rubbed with salt to speed up the process of drying, most kokum will retain a little crystalline powder which can be mistaken for mold, however a quick rinse before adding the rind to a dish will remove the residue. A souring agent, kokum can be used to naturally tenderize meats in a marinade and in Goa it is incorporated into rich fish curries. Add some to rhubarb, apple, and cinnamon during stewing to enhance the flavor of any lime or lemon present in the dish.
Use: with allspice, coriander seeds, cumin seeds, cinnamon, cassia, cloves, fennel seeds, paprika, turmeric, and star anise.

Look for: evenly colored large pieces and check for foreign matter such as small stones.
Store: in a cool, dry cupboard for up to 2 years.

MACE

See Nutmeg and mace

MAHLAB

Hard to come by, mahlab is the husked kernel of the wild black cherry and is a native of southern Europe. With a scent much like marzipan, it has lovely undertones of cherry and blossoms coupled with a nutty, slightly bitter taste. It is used in cakes and pastries throughout the Middle East as well as in sweet and savory European dishes. Correct storage is important as mahlab will permeate other spices if not well sealed in an airtight container.

Use: with allspice, cardamom, chili, cinnamon, cloves, coriander, cumin, fennel, fenugreek, ginger, paprika, star anise, tamarind, and turmeric.
Look for: whole kernels as ground discolors quickly.
Store: away from light and humidity for up to 1 year.

MUSTARD SEEDS

Yellow, black, and brown mustard seeds are pressed to make mustard oil, then processed to make spreadable mustard and mustard powder. A very old spice, mustard was originally used for medicinal purposes (as an internal stimulant and diuretic and for muscle strains). Although belonging to the hot flavor group, mustard seeds have no discernable aroma as whole seeds or in ground form, however they contain an enzyme which is activated by liquid. Incredibly versatile, mustard seeds can be used in Indian curries, pickles, salad dressings, and meat seasonings.

Use: with allspice, cardamom, chili, cinnamon, cloves, coriander, cumin, fennel, fenugreek, ginger, paprika, star anise, tamarind, and turmeric.
Look for: seeds which are free of debris.
Store: whole mustard seeds for up to 4 years.

NIGELLA

Native to western Asia and southern Europe, it grows very well today in Egypt, the Middle East, and India. A member of the pungent flavor group, nigella is sometimes mistaken for black cumin, however it is quite different in that it has a nutty, metallic, somewhat peppery taste and is often used for garnishing breads.

Use: with allspice, cardamom, coriander, cumin, fennel, fenugreek, galangal, mustard seeds, paprika, star anise, tamarind, and turmeric.
Look for: seeds that are uniformly black.
Store: in a cool, dry place for up to 3 years.

NUTMEG AND MACE

Native to the Banda Islands in Indonesia, nutmeg and mace have long been expensive spices. These spices are literally inseparable in that they come from the same fruit, which looks like a small nectarine. The musky orange-colored mace blade comprises the embryo nutmeg which must be carefully removed and dried before use. The fruit itself is of little value but is used by some to create pickles. Mace blades are a member of the pungent flavor group and are used in slow-cooked meat dishes, in shellfish and fish soup stocks, terrines, and pickling spices. Nutmeg, on the other hand, belongs to the sweet flavor group and is used in classic puddings and sweets. It is also wonderful grated over roasted root vegetables, cooked spinach, and in the slow-cooked pasta meat sauces of Italy and Spain.

Use mace: with cloves, paprika, and black pepper.
Use nutmeg: with allspice, cinnamon, cloves, and ginger.
Look for mace: blades that are still reasonably intact, bright orange in color and rich in aroma.
Look for nutmeg: whole, light brown color with no visible insect or worm holes.
Store mace: for up to 1 year if whole but once ground for a maximum of 6 months.
Store nutmeg: whole up to 2 years and ground for 6 months.

PAPRIKA

An amalgamating spice, paprika comes in many types and grades. Grown in climates where the fruit can benefit from sufficient sunlight, paprika was first used by the Mexican Indians. Over the years it has gained great popularity, particularly in Hungary where the national dish of goulash contains mild paprika. Spain has also cultivated an array of dishes in which paprika is the star. Spanish paprika can be used in many dishes, instantly adding a smoky note. Marinades and sauces, terrines, meat pastries and grilled meats are all improved with a teaspoon of paprika. Paprika combines well with all spices and is also very compatible with most herbs. Look for even color and texture.

Use: with allspice, cinnamon, cloves, coriander, cumin, fennel, ginger, and turmeric.
Look for: even color and texture.
Store: ground in a cool, dry place for up to 1 year.

PEPPER

There are many varieties of pepper, but the most common are black, white, green, pink, and Szechuan. All are part of the hot flavor group.

- Pink – The pink peppercorn is not actually a pepper but rather a dried berry from the *Schinus ariera* tree. Commonly used in fish dishes of the Mediterranean, rich meat terrines, and salad dressings, it combines with most herbs as well as allspice, coriander seeds, chili, and fennel seeds. It is most commonly found bottled in brine or dried.

- Szechuan – Szechuan pepper has a fragrant aroma and slight lemony flavor. Its culinary use originated in India around 100 BC. Coming from the prickly ash tree, the leaves can also be eaten and are known as sansho. Unusually, it is the husk that imparts flavor so it is important to remove the small black seeds from inside the husk before grinding. Szechwan combines with allspice, chili, fennel seeds, ginger, juniper, paprika, and star anise.

- Vine pepper – A climber that grows wild in its native southern India and Java. Each spike may have 50 or more single peppercorns that begin green and ripen to yellow and finally red pink when they are fully ripe. Black peppercorns are green peppercorns that have been picked and dried. White peppercorns result from removing the outer layer of skin where all the oils reside. Most commonly used as a table condiment, black pepper is suitable added to almost everything. Green peppercorns still on the vine are often much tastier than the dried varieties. They are used for marinades and curry pastes as well as in classic terrine and pâté applications. The mildness of white peppercorns works well in sauces. All vine peppers combine well with all spices and herbs but, if brined, rinse well so the brining agents do not disturb the flavor of your dish too much.

POPPY SEEDS

Native to the Middle East, the poppy has been cultivated for over 3,000 years due to its medicinal applications. A member of the amalgamating flavor group, the seeds are used mostly as a decorative garnish. White poppy seeds are also available but not commonly seen.

Use: with allspice, cassia, cinnamon, cloves, ginger, green cardamom, sesame seeds, sumac, and coriander seeds.

Look for: even colored seeds and no debris.

Store: in a cool, dry cupboard for up to 3 years.

SAFFRON

The trade history surrounding this much-lauded member of the pungent flavor group is long and intriguing. Cleopatra is said to have washed her face in saffron water daily and over the years it has been one of the most falsified spices on the market. The real thing comes from the stamens of *Crocus sativus* which must be harvested in the dawn light over a short period, usually only about 3 weeks. The flavor and distinctive aroma of saffron only appears once the stamens are dried when they are graded according to quality. Paella and risotto are great applications, as are the desserts and grain-based dishes of the Middle East.

Use: with all other spices but in moderation.

Look for: long, dark amber, fleshy-looking strands.

Store: in small quantities away from light, heat and moisture for up to 6 months.

SESAME SEEDS

Native to Indonesia and Africa, sesame is reputedly the oldest crop grown for oil production. To this day the seeds continue to be used as a garnish for bread and in the Middle East they are used extensively in their whole state as well as ground to create halva and tahini. Black sesame is simply the unhulled version and is found in Asian dishes more so than white. An amalgamating spice, sesame seeds have a delicious nutty flavor.

Use: with sumac, paprika, nutmeg, ginger, coriander seeds, cloves, cinnamon and cassia, green cardamom, and allspice.

Look for: even size and color. No debris.

Store: hulled seeds for up to 9 months and black seeds for up to 2 years provided the husks are not broken.

STAR ANISE

Strong and sweet with a liquorice pungency, star anise has a distinct scent and taste that has long been popular, particularly in Chinese cuisine – it is the dominant spice in the Chinese five-spice mix. It is native to south and south-west China and north Vietnam and is harvested when green, then dried in the sun. After being introduced to Europe in the 16th century, its essential oils were soon discovered. Released through steam distillation the oils soon became a flavoring agent for sweets and liqueurs. Its spiky form can make it difficult to handle, but powdered star anise can lose its flavor quickly, especially if not stored away from light and heat. Whole star anise can be added to soups and slow-cooked meat dishes, but must be removed before serving.

Use: with allspice, cardamom, chili, cinnamon, cloves, coriander, cumin, fennel, ginger, mace, and nutmeg.

Look for: unbroken star anise.

Store: in a cool, dry cupboard for up to 3 years.

SUMAC

The dried berry of a small shrub that grows wild throughout the Middle East and Mediterranean, sumac was used in Roman times before they discovered lemons. The leaves of the shrub are used in spice mixes such as *za'atar* while the young shoots have long been used to create dye. The American Indians used sumac berries to make a refreshing drink. A member of the tangy flavor group, sumac has natural souring abilities that can be used anywhere that a lemon would be called for. It is a great meat tenderizer, with fish it is the lemon you don't need to squeeze, and in salad dressing it gives an extra attractive color. Whole seeds are difficult to come by, but if available can be added to dishes in muslin bags and removed before serving.

Use: with chili, ginger, paprika, sesame seeds, and herbs such as oregano and rosemary.

Look for: evenly ground sumac of a deep pinky-red color.

Store: in an airtight container away from light and heat to avoid lumps forming for up to 1 year.

TAMARIND

A natural souring agent, tamarind can be bought cheaply in a compressed block form. It is native to the tropical lands of East Africa but also grows wild throughout Asia. Many parts of the tree are used for cooking, including the pod-like fruit. Also appreciated for its medicinal properties, tamarind is said to work wonders on the liver as a natural cleanser. Tamarind water is sold in parts of Asia on street corners as a refreshing drink. Tamarind is also used to create sweets, pickles, sauces, and Worcestershire sauce. It is a great tenderizer for meat marinades, for adding a tang to South-east Asian soups, pickles and chutneys and curry pastes. A member of the tangy flavor group, it works with most spices.

Use: with cumin, coriander, kaffir lime leaves, and star anise.

Look for: either compressed block or in a liquid form.

Store: well wrapped in the pantry to avoid it drying out for a maximum of 1 year.

TURMERIC

Most commonly seen in its powdered form, turmeric is part of the ginger family and belongs to the amalgamating flavor group. It is indigenous to South-east Asia where it has long been used for culinary and medicinal applications. Musky with a bitter edge, turmeric has a flavor all of its own and due to its extraordinary staining ability, is used commercially as a coloring agent for food.

Use: fresh, where possible, in conjunction with the intense-flavored herbs used in South-east Asian cooking.

Look for: brightly colored plump fresh turmeric – not wrinkled or dry. Even-colored ground turmeric.

Store: fresh in a dry place where it will keep for several weeks; ground in an airtight, preferably glass, container away from heat, moisture, and light.

VANILLA

The vanilla pod is produced by the tropical climbing orchid that grows wild in its native Central America and Mexico. However, another variety in a smaller form grows readily in Tahiti where it is harvested and also sold on the international market. In both cases the hand-fertilized flowers bear green beans or pods that, after picking, are dried in kilns repeatedly over a six-month period until the desired state is reached. This time-consuming process can result in pods being handled over 100 times before being dispatched for sale. Part of the sweet flavor group, vanilla can easily dominate a dish if not used carefully.

Use: with allspice, cassia, cinnamon, cloves, ginger, green cardamom, sesame seeds, nutmeg, and star anise.

Look for: thick plump pods with no sign of moisture.

Store: in pod form in an airtight jar for up to 1 year.

Additional Glossary

ARROWROOT
A gluten-free, easy-to-digest thickening agent made from the tuber of a plant native to the rainforests of the West Indies. Available from all general supermarkets.

BLACK BEANS
Fermented and salted soy beans, black beans are probably most commonly associated with Cantonese cuisine's black bean sauce. They have a very intense musky tone which can be overpowering, so use sparingly. The beans are best purchased whole and salted rather than in a pre-prepared sauce form. Simply wash the required amount in a bowl, rubbing the beans together between your fingers to remove the outer skin. Rinse well in cold water then pat dry and squash using the side of a knife on a chopping board to make a paste then add to other ingredients to make a marinade.

BLACK CLOUD EAR FUNGUS (ALSO CLOUD EAR, MOUSE EAR, AND JELLY MUSHROOM FUNGUS)
Resembling seaweed or a piece of leather, this fungus can be purchased both fresh and dried. If dried, simply rehydrate overnight in a large quantity of cold water. Once softened, remove the core of the fungus which can be quite chewy and fibrous. Slice the remainder very finely and use uncooked in salads or stir-fries (which gives it a lovely crunchy texture). Larger pieces can be steamed along with dried shitake mushrooms and Asian greens. Black ear is valued by the Chinese for its medicinal properties as it is believed to improve circulation. Dried fungus can be stored for up to a year in a dry place.

CHINESE GREENS (BOK CHOY, CHINESE CABBAGE, GAI LARN, AND ONG CHOY)
Up until relatively recently bok choy was the only widely available Chinese vegetable. Several varieties can now be found in most supermarkets, however, all with slightly different textures and tastes. Firmer, stalkier varieties like gai larn are best stir-fried with meat on the bone and enjoyed for their slightly bitter undertones. Softer-leafed varieties, on the other hand, like bok choy, are lovely in soups and stir-fries alongside the softer-textured chicken and fish. Unlike many other vegetables, the stems are the choicest part of Chinese greens.

CURRY LEAVES
Native to Sri Lanka and India, these leaves have a strong, bitter flavor. Purchase fresh from good specialty stores. Leave to dry out thoroughly before packing into a jar for storing. Leaves will keep for 6 months before they begin to lose their distinctive savory flavor.

DAIKON
A large white root vegetable used throughout Asia and known for its digestive qualities. With a texture similar to a turnip, but far tastier, it is most often shredded and served raw alongside sashimi, pickled and used in sushi or stir-fried. It is available in most general supermarkets. High in Vitamin C, all parts of the plant are enjoyed throughout Asia including the seeds, leaves, and root.

GRAPESEED OIL
With a high burning point, no aroma or taste, this versatile oil is ideal for both shallow- and deep-frying as it will never taint or influence the flavor of other ingredients. A by-product of the wine industry and much cheaper than olive oil, grapeseed oil is a must-have staple in your pantry, ideal for all cooking. Look for it at specialty food stores and major supermarkets.

KAFFIR LIME LEAVES
Fruit from the kaffir lime tree produce almost no juice at all, yet their thick perfumed skin and figure-eight-shaped leaves are essential to Thai cuisine. Kaffir is used in conjunction with spices from other flavor groups to bring a sort of harmony to a dish and it is often used in dishes alongside coconut milk, galangal, cilantro, and chili. More readily available in fresh form, dried leaves are also widely available from Asian supermarkets. Simply soak them in warm water for 10 minutes prior to slicing and adding to marinades and soups.

LAVASH BREAD
A thin baked bread dough. Rolled out to the thickness of a wafer or cracker, it is much more crisp than conventional bread. A great accompaniment to dips and spreads but also very good on its own, lavash bread is easily obtained from specialty food stores and delicatessens.

LEMONGRASS
This aromatic grass grows wild in both South-east Asia and Latin America but it is Asia that has embraced this woody perennial into its cuisine wholeheartedly. Available from all good grocery stores, it is best used fresh when the roots are still attached so the flavor is still zesty and sharp. Also available bottled and sliced (though fresh is definitely far superior). Fresh lemongrass can be stored but must be well wrapped. Remove the outer leaves of the bulb itself before use as they are very tough. Use the inner white part of the plant, sliced finely across the bulb.

LOTUS ROOT
From the beautiful flowering water plant of the same name and used in both sweet and savory dishes. An edible rhizome of grey brown color which grows in sausage-like links. Young, tender roots can be added to salads while more mature sections are best eaten stir-fried, in soups or stuffed and fried. Crunchy and a little fibrous, lotus has a subtle flavor of its own which makes it a perfect partner for many other more strongly flavored ingredients.

Purchase pre-sliced in segments (to show off the lacy pattern inside the root) and frozen from Asian supermarkets. Look in the dried section for both slices and pieces. Rehydrate by soaking in cold water for several hours and then slice as needed.

MARSALA
An Italian low-alcohol liquor made from grapes. Sweet and syrupy, it is used in cooking much the same as sherry or other sweet wines. The alternative cremova Marsala has the addition of egg (more often used for cooking than as a beverage). Marsala can be purchased at good liquor stores.

MAHLAB
Renowned for its taste, the black cherry is used throughout the Middle East in both savory and sweet dishes. However,

also prized is the pit of the black cherry which is removed, dried and then ground to a powder which texturally resembles almond flour or meal. It has a very distinctive marzipan taste and is common in breads and sweets throughout Turkey and the Middle East.

MIRIN

Also known as sweet rice wine, it is used exclusively for cooking with the exception of one day per year during the festive New Year period in Japan when it is flavored with spices and sipped from ceremonial cups. Look for those that are labeled as *hon-mirin* as these have been naturally brewed rather than the *aji-mirin* which has the addition of additives. A unique, gentle flavor, it serves as the base of teriyaki sauce. Available from all Asian supermarkets, it is a good staple to have in the pantry for marinades and glazes.

MUSCOVADO SUGAR

Available from major supermarkets in both light and dark varieties. The key is to look for sugar that is unrefined which has a much richer molasses-like flavor due to the natural cane molasses. Use the light sugar for general baking and the dark kind for anything with nuts, dates, and ginger.

NAM PRIK PAO

A flavoring agent also used as an accompaniment to Southeast Asian dishes. Sometimes referred to as chili jam, it can be either cooked or uncooked and generally consists of sugar, rice vinegar, chili, salt, tamarind paste, and soy bean paste. Add to a chicken marinade for extra flavor or thin down with a little soy and sesame oils to make a fast dipping sauce. Available from Asian supermarkets.

ONION BOLTS

The top of the sprouting onion with the flower cut off, it tastes like chives crossed with onion. They should be available from Asian grocery stores. However, if not available, they can be replaced with spring onion bottoms.

ORANGE BLOSSOM WATER

Has become a little more well-known since rose water became a staple of many cooks' kitchens. Distilled in the same manner as rose water, the flavor of orange blossom is bright, fresh, and crisp. It can overwhelm easily though so a teaspoon or two is generally all that is called for. Purchase at all good delicatessens and specialty food stores.

PLANTAIN

Similar to a banana in looks and taste. Naturally very starchy, plantains are used for their thickening qualities in many Pacific Island dishes as well as in Latin America. Look for those that are ripe for cooking as a green, unripe plaintain can be hard and bitter-tasting.

RED RICE (ALSO CAMARGUE RICE)

Has an appearance not too dissimilar to wild rice. Still retaining its exterior husk, red rice has a great deal more nutritious value than polished white rice. Nutty in flavor, red rice can be combined with white rice for an attractive appearance. Red rice doesn't take as long to cook as white rice, however, so bear that in mind when cooking. Available from specialty food stores.

ROSE WATER

Traditionally used to make Turkish delight or *loukoumi* as well as a thirst-quenching beverage for Eastern nobility, it was also used to plump dried figs and dates before serving. Readily available from all good specialty food stores, it is naturally distilled and strong in flavor.

SERRANO HAM (ALSO JAMON)

Best described as the Spanish equivalent of Italian prosciutto. An air-dried meat, it has quite a recognizably different flavor to its Italian cousin. Becoming more readily available through specialty food stores and delicatessens, it may be more expensive than prosciutto but it's worth it.

SHAO-HSING WINE

Yellow in hue and rather toxic, this Chinese rice wine has a similar taste to sherry. In cooking applications it is used most commonly in stir-fries and marinades. When consumed as a drink, it is always served slightly warmed. Available from most Asian supermarkets and some specialty food stores.

SHITAKE MUSHROOMS

Perhaps the best known of the Asian fungus group, these small woody mushrooms are best bought dried and rehydrated for cooking as the flavor is much more pronounced once dried. Vital to so many classic Cantonese recipes as well as the cuisines of Japan and South-east Asia, these little mushrooms add intense flavor. They are available sliced and dried from major supermarkets.

SOY SAUCE

Available in both Japanese and Chinese varieties (and both have quite different flavors from each other). Soy is a staple of Asia created from roasted wheat, ground soy beans, salt, and a mold starter. It is fermented and aged in order to mellow the flavor. It is very important to look for a narurally brewed soy sauce as imitations are unusually thick and dark-coloured with a strong flavor that can easily ruin a dish. The two categories of soy are light and dark. Light is thinner, saltier and can be used for many more dishes than the darker, thicker, more intensely flavored variety. Light soy sauce is best used for the majority of dishes with dark soy sauce more suitable for red meats and heavily flavored dishes.

TAGINE

A cooking vessel used throughout the Middle East to create a sort of stew. The conical shape lid of the tagine traps steam from the cooking process inside the vessel ensuring the dish remains moist. Almost anything can be cooked in a tagine – specialty dishes vary from place to place. Tagines can be purchased at specialty food stores and kitchenware stores.

TAHINI

Made from ground sesame seeds and used extensively throughout the Middle East for flavoring, adding to marinades and as a thickening agent. Available both hulled and unhulled, tahini has a wonderful flavor of sesame that is also great eaten as a butter substitute on toast or mixed with honey for a sweet treat.

Additional Glossary

✻ Index

🦁 Acknowledgements

A huge thank you to the wonderful team at Nest on Ponsonby Road, for the beautiful kitchenware that appears throughout the book. Thanks to Arabesque on Ponsonby Road for the gorgeous items that feature in the 'Spiced Nights' chapter. Thanks also to Iko Iko on K Road, Cheri at Ruby & Sol in Grey Lynn for additional props.

PERSONAL THANKS – MH

My endless thanks go to my parents, Kevin and Elaine, for their support and help, not just in regard to this book but for all the years I've been around.

To Jacqui, whose photography has made this book a true thing of beauty surpassing my wildest dreams.

To Lisa, Miss B and Mr R, for all those recipes that had to be eaten and tested. Without you three, my life would be far less rewarding.

To Cathy and Peter, for being the most relaxed people I know on the planet.

To Saul, for the endless amusement but also the honesty you bring to my life.

To the Farro team, thank you for your enthusiasm, help and pep talks over the months.

To Vespa, for being my writing companion and helper.

To Joel and Charmaine, Nathan and Jamie, for your support and enthusiasm.

Finally, thank you to Keely for the design and to Louise and the team at New Holland for giving me this opportunity.

PERSONAL THANKS – JB

Thank you to the gifted Michal Haines for creating these delicious dishes that were a pleasure to photograph.

Thank you to photographer Hannah Richards for your generosity and camaraderie.

Thank you to Greg Blanchard for your big-hearted support of my career, which has included many pep talks over the years!

Thank you to Keely O'Shannessy our talented and dedicated designer. You make us look good!

A big thank you to Louise Armstrong our wonderful editor. Your hard work does not go unappreciated. Thank you for the opportunity – you're the best!

Much appreciation to Belinda Cooke and the rest of the publishing team.

First American edition published in 2009 by
Interlink Books
An imprint of Interlink Publishing Group, Inc.
46 Crosby Street, Northampton, MA 01060
www.interlinkbooks.com

ISBN: 978-1-56656-754-1

Commissioned and project managed by Louise Armstrong
Cover design by Juliana Spear
Edited by Renée Lang
American edition edited by Hiltrud Schulz, Sara Rauch and Leyla Moushabeck

10 9 8 7 6 5 4 3 2 1

Color reproduction by SC (Sang Choy) International Pte Ltd, Singapore
Printed in China by SNP Leefung